About Island Press

Since 1984, the nonprofit organization Island Press has been stimulating, shaping, and communicating ideas that are essential for solving environmental problems worldwide. With more than 1,000 titles in print and some 30 new releases each year, we are the nation's leading publisher on environmental issues. We identify innovative thinkers and emerging trends in the environmental field. We work with world-renowned experts and authors to develop cross-disciplinary solutions to environmental challenges.

Island Press designs and executes educational campaigns, in conjunction with our authors, to communicate their critical messages in print, in person, and online using the latest technologies, innovative programs, and the media. Our goal is to reach targeted audiences—scientists, policy makers, environmental advocates, urban planners, the media, and concerned citizens—with information that can be used to create the framework for long-term ecological health and human well-being.

Island Press gratefully acknowledges major support from The Bobolink Foundation, Caldera Foundation, The Curtis and Edith Munson Foundation, The Forrest C. and Frances H. Lattner Foundation, The JPB Foundation, The Kresge Foundation, The Summit Charitable Foundation, Inc., and many other generous organizations and individuals.

The opinions expressed in this book are those of the author(s) and do not necessarily reflect the views of our supporters.

NEW MOBILITIES

New Mobilities

Smart Planning for Emerging Transportation Technologies

Todd Litman

⬤ ISLANDPRESS | Washington | Covelo

Library of Congress Control Number: 2020947610

All Island Press books are printed on environmentally responsible materials.

Manufactured in the United States of America
10 9 8 7 6 5 4 3 2 1

Keywords: active travel, air taxis, automobile dependency, autonomous vehicles, aviation innovation, bicycling, cargo bike, drone, electric bicycle, electric scooter, integrated navigation and transport payment apps, logistics management, micromobility, microtransit, Mobility as a Service (MaaS), mobility prioritization, multimodal, network connectivity, pneumatic tube transport, public transportation innovations, resource-efficient travel, ridehailing, Smart Growth, telework, supersonic jet, transportation demand management (TDM), tunnel roads, vehicle sharing

MIX
Paper from responsible sources
FSC® C008955
FSC
www.fsc.org

To build houses, carpenters require nails, and to produce bread, bakers require flour. To help produce a better future world, planners require diverse and reliable data. The analysis in this book is built on many data sources, including, for example, a 1901 US Department of Commerce survey of 2,567 "workingmen's families" annual expenditures, divided into eighteen categories. Discovering such obscure information is exciting and humbling. I marvel at the dedication of the government researchers who visited hundreds of households, inquiring about their incomes and shopping patterns, and carefully compiling the results into tidy rows and columns, to help researchers better understand our complex world. More than a century later, this musty information provided key insights concerning how past planning decisions affected lower-income households' transportation cost burdens.

I therefore dedicate this book to the countless workers who diligently collect and organize the data used for planning research. Thank you for your important but often underappreciated efforts!

I also dedicate this book to my wife, Shoshana, whose support for my work is beyond measure.

CONTENTS

We are embarking on a journey, a quest, to find our best transportation future. We are in this together. I will try to be good company.

Like any good quest, our journey involves both practical challenges and deeper issues. At a practical level, we will critically evaluate how emerging transportation technologies and services will affect our lives and communities, with a healthy dose of skepticism toward some optimistic claims. To do this we will examine the impacts of previous transportation technologies and investigate concepts such as *efficiency, equity,* and *freedom.*

I am a policy analyst, which means that my research integrates physical design and economics plus political and legal analysis. My work tends to expand the scope of impacts and options considered in planning to include a broader range of modes and solutions than normally considered in transportation planning.

I love research. My research is sometimes criticized as "anti-car," but that is unfair. It is true that my analysis tends to consider often-overlooked costs of automobile travel and often overlooked benefits of multimodal transportation; however, I certainly recognize that motorized transportation provides many benefits, and automobiles are the most appropriate mode for many trips. Put briefly, I advocate a balanced transportation diet, so each mode can be used for what it does best. We will see how this philosophy applies to the New Mobilities.

This book could have been written as a "gee whiz!" celebration of emerging transportation technologies, or conversely, it could have been an exposé of the problems they will create and the exaggerations of their proponents. It is neither. Instead, I try to provide comprehensive and objective analysis of the New Mobilities' benefits and costs and the roles they should play in our future lives.

From Car Enthusiast to Multimodal Advocate

I am a recovering car enthusiast. Like most baby boom generation guys, I grew up loving cars, particularly sporty imports. I savored their look, sound, and smell. I obtained my driver's license at age sixteen, and during the next two years went through a 1960 Fiat (I burned out the engine), a 1958 Saab (I burned out the engine), and a 1957 Volkswagen (I sold it to a friend). I used beautiful chrome tools to adjust tappets and replace leaky oil seals. Of course, I had to work after school every day to afford them, leaving little time for sports or socializing, and I cringe at my irresponsible and sometimes dangerous driving behavior. Thank goodness I survived!

The truth is, I was a slave to these vehicles: I worked to pay for cars so I could drive to work. I attained freedom when I sold the Volkswagen to finance a half-year backpacking trip around Latin America, where I traveled by foot, truck, bus, train, boat, and airplane through a dozen countries. Once back in North America, I relied on walking, bicycling, and public transit. We owned cars when our children were young but have been without a vehicle for the last decade, and the resulting savings financed their university educations. Car-free living made our family healthy, wealthy, and wise.

These experiences help me appreciate diverse mobility options, including New Mobilities. During the last decade I've enjoyed using an increasing variety of travel modes including e-bikes and e-scooters, carshare services, high-speed trains, and teleconferencing programs, plus various navigation and fare payment apps. These are all part of an efficient and equitable mobility system.

But this book is not about me; it is about you and your community: when it comes to transportation, we're all in this together!

ACKNOWLEDGMENTS

I greatly appreciate the assistance provided for this project by Rob Bernhardt, Dan Burden, Stuart Culbertson, Stuart Donovan, Sharon Feigon, Elliot Fishman, Shoshana Litman, Cameron Owens, Gregg Sheehy, Sam Starr, Paul Zykofsky, and my editor, Heather Boyer. I would also like to express appreciation to my many friends and colleagues whose research has contributed to and inspired this book, including Asha Weinstein Agrawal, Emily Badger, Marlon G. Boarnet, Ralph Buehler, Daniel G. Chatman, Joe Cortright, Ahmed M. El-Geneidy, Reid Ewing, Yingling Fan, Larry Frank, Norman Garrick, Aaron Golub, Erick Guerra, Shima Hamidi, Susan Handy, Eric Jaffe, Jeff Kenworthy, Kara Kockelman, Ugo Lachapelle, Nico Larco, Jonathan Levine, David Levinson, Michael Lewyn, Michael Manville, Nancy McGuckin, Michael West Mehaffy, Greg Marsden, Karel Martens, Adam Millard-Ball, Peter Newman, Robert B. Noland, Stephanie Pollack, Robert Puentes, Caroline Rodier, Bruce Schaller, Marc Schlossberg, Susan Shaheen, Gregory H. Shill, Donald Shoup, Michael Sivak, Jeff Speck, Daniel Sperling, Sam Schwartz, Paul Tranter, Jarrett Walker, Ben Welle, Steve Winkelman, and Lloyd Wright. Thank you all!

Chapter 1

Introduction

If you are shopping for an automobile, you'll find an abundance of useful information. Numerous websites, magazines, and reports provide practical guidance for evaluating and comparing makes and models. These sources offer detailed information, concerning costs, dimensions, performance, and features, plus ratings and reviews by experts and amateurs. This helps shoppers make informed decisions.

However, if you are trying to evaluate emerging transportation technologies and services, you'll find much less useful information. Although many websites, magazines, and reports describe these new transportation options, their content is generally less helpful. Most sources consider just a few modes, provide limited information, and are biased. It can be difficult to find comprehensive and objective information on their impacts, or practical guidance for incorporating them into your community's transportation future.

I wrote this book to help fill that gap. It provides the equivalent of product reviews for twelve *New Mobilities*, the emerging transportation modes and services listed in Table 1-1. These were selected because they are currently developing and likely to become more important in the future.

The New Mobilities have tantalizing potential. They allow people to scoot, ride, and fly like never before. They can provide large and diverse benefits. However, they can also impose significant costs on users and communities. Decision-makers need detailed information on their impacts.

1

Table 1-1 New Mobilities Considered in this Book. This book critically evaluates these twelve emerging transportation technologies and services.

Active Travel and Micromobilities. Walking, bicycling, and variations, including small, lower-speed motorized vehicles such as electric scooters, bikes, and cargo bikes.

Vehicle Sharing. Convenient and affordable bicycle, scooter, and automobile rental services.

Ridehailing and Microtransit. Mobility services that transport individuals and small groups.

Electric Vehicles. Battery-powered scooters, bikes, cars, trucks, and buses.

Autonomous Vehicles. Vehicles that can operate without a human driver. Also called self-driving vehicles.

Public Transport Innovations. Innovations that improve transit travel convenience, comfort, safety, and speed.

Mobility as a Service (MaaS). Navigation and transport payment apps that integrate multiple modes.

Telework. Telecommunications that substitute for physical travel.

Tunnel Roads and Pneumatic Tube Transport. Underground road and high-speed tube transport networks.

Aviation Innovation. Air taxis, drones, and supersonic jets.

Mobility Prioritization. Pricing systems and incentives that favor higher-value trips and more efficient modes.

Logistics Management. Integrated freight delivery services.

This book's goal is to provide practical guidance for optimizing these emerging technologies and services. It critically evaluates their benefits and costs, examines how they can affect our lives and communities, and discusses how we should prepare in order to maximize their benefits and minimize their costs. It is intended to help you determine whether they should be mandated, encouraged, regulated, restricted, or forbidden in a particular situation. It considers a wider range of goals and perspectives, and applies more comprehensive and systematic analysis, than other comparable publications.

This is a timely issue. Transportation planning decisions affect virtually every aspect of our lives. In the future, households and communities will face countless decisions concerning how to respond to these emerging technologies and services. It is important to make informed decisions based on comprehensive analysis.

Better Planning for a Better World

Much of human progress results from transportation innovations—from walking to wagons, boats, stagecoaches, steamships, trains, automobiles, airplanes, and space travel. New transportation technologies and services expanded our world, extending where we can work, trade, and play, which increased our productivity and improved our lives in countless ways. This progress hasn't stopped; more innovations are currently under development, from e-scooters to autonomous cars and from navigation apps to e-medicine. What comes next? Moving sidewalks? Jet packs? Flying buses? What problems might they create? How should we prepare?

The twentieth century was the period of *automobile ascendency*, during which private motor vehicle travel grew, to the detriment of other modes, to dominate our transportation systems and our communities. During the twenty-first century we are likely to see more *transportation system diversity*. Integrated information technologies will allow travelers to easily navigate myriad connected mobility options. If we are smart, the results will be far more convenient, affordable, inclusive, efficient, healthy, and fun than what we have now.

Of course, predicting the future is fraught with uncertainty. According to forecasts made a few decades ago, current travel should involve moving sidewalks, jet packs, and flying cars, with space travel a common occurrence.[1] General Motors' 1939 World's Fair *Futurama* display predicted that by the 1960s, uncongested, 100-mile-per-hour superhighways would provide seamless travel between suburban homes and towering cities in luxurious, streamlined cars. A 1961 *Weekend Magazine* article predicted that by 2000, "Rocket belts will increase a man's stride to 30 feet, and bus-type helicopters will travel along crowded air skyways. There will be moving plastic-covered pavements, individual hoppicopters, and 200 mph monorail trains operating in all large cities. The family car will be soundless, vibrationless and self-propelled thermostatically. The engine will be smaller than a typewriter. Cars will travel overland on an 18 inch air cushion."[2]

The 1969 *Plan for New York City* stated, "It is assumed that new technology will be enlisted in this improved transportation system, including transit powered by gravity and vacuum and mechanical aids to pedestrian movement, such as moving belts or quick-access shuttle vehicles. These devices almost surely will become available by the end of the century."

How accurate were these predictions? Where's your rocket belt? Did you travel today on a moving-belt sidewalk, vacuum-powered transit, or hoppicopter? Most predictions failed, not because the technology is infeasible, but because our priorities changed. Past predictions assumed that our goal is to travel faster, farther, and with less physical effort. In reality, travelers are equally concerned with convenience, comfort, affordability, and health. We often choose slower modes that offer these attributes—for example, walking to local shops rather than driving to regional shopping centers for cost savings, exercise, and enjoyment.

We *could* travel faster if we were willing to spend more money. In the 1960s motorists paid about four times current inflation-adjusted fuel taxes to finance highway building. Had citizens supported large tax increases or road tolls, we could have even more high-speed highways than we do now. However, there is little public support for new highway investments. Similarly, in the 1960s, governments spent billions of dollars to develop supersonic commercial jets. Concorde supersonic service operated on a few routes between 1997 and 2003, but too few travelers were willing to pay significantly higher fares to save a few hours on intercontinental trips, resulting in the project's demise.

A new planning paradigm is changing the way we define transportation problems and evaluate potential solutions, in order to better respond to consumer preferences. The old paradigm assumed that our primary goal is to increase mobility. This view favored faster but expensive modes, such as automobiles and air travel, over slower, more affordable and resource-efficient modes such as walking, bicycling, and public transit. A new paradigm recognizes other community goals, such as affordability, social equity, and public health, as well as other perspectives, including the travel demands of people who cannot, should not, or prefer not to drive. The new transportation planning paradigm requires comprehensive and multimodal planning.

New technologies expand the scope of what we *can* do, but communities must determine what we *should* do. The New Mobilities can help create a better future, but their benefits are contingent; they depend on how we incorporate them into our communities. Mobility is both precious and dangerous, not to be wasted or abused. If we are smart, these new modes and services can help make the world more efficient and fair. If we are foolish, they can increase waste and inequity. *Heaven or hell: it's up to us.*

Table 1-2 Impacts and Perspectives. Conventional transportation planning considers a limited set of impacts and perspectives. This analysis considers additional factors.

Conventional Analysis	Additional Factors Considered in this Book
Government infrastructure expenditures	Downstream and indirect traffic impacts
Traffic speed and congestion delays	User experience (convenience and comfort)
Vehicle operating costs (fuel, tolls, tire wear)	Total user costs and affordability (costs to lower-income users)
Per-mile crash rates	Parking congestion and facility costs
Pollution emissions rates	Mobility for non-drivers
	Social equity impacts (impacts on disadvantaged groups)
	Barrier effect (delay to pedestrians and cyclists)
	Per capita crash risk
	Per capita resource consumption and pollution emissions
	Public fitness and health
	Contagion risk
	Additional environmental impacts (e.g., embodied energy and impervious surface coverage)
	Impacts on strategic planning goals

Some optimists predict that New Mobilities will solve our transportation problems, but there are reasons to be skeptical. For example, proponents claim that shared, autonomous, electric vehicles can virtually eliminate traffic congestion, crash risk, and pollution and will be so cheap that they can be financed by advertising.[3] However, such optimistic predictions overlook many costs and risks. These vehicles will be appropriate for some trips but not others. To be efficient and equitable, our future transportation system must be diverse and provide transportation demand management (TDM) incentives to encourage travelers to choose the most appropriate mode for each trip: walking and bicycling for local travel, large-capacity public transit on major urban corridors, and automobiles when they are truly most efficient, considering all impacts.

New Mobilities raise many planning questions. For example, numerous studies indicate that micromobilities (bicycles, scooters, and e-bikes) can provide consumer savings, infrastructure savings, and improved public health and environmental quality.[4] More than half of all North American trips are less than three miles in length, a perfect distance for these modes. One Dutch survey found that people who purchase an e-bike reduce their vehicle mileage about 10 percent.[5] The potential benefits are huge! How much should communities invest in these modes? Should roads be redesigned to improve micromobility safety? Should cities reduce automobile parking minimums and require parking for scooters and bikes? Should we provide incentives to use these modes instead of automobiles for local trips?

Is it time to change our planning goals? To reduce traffic problems, including congestion, crash risk, and air pollution, many jurisdictions have established vehicle travel reduction targets and are implementing TDM and Smart Growth policies to help achieve them. Do autonomous electric vehicles eliminate the need for vehicle travel reduction policies? Alternatively, should communities favor the New Mobilities that reduce total vehicle travel and discourage those that don't?

Consider another issue. To significantly reduce traffic congestion and pollution emissions, autonomous vehicles will require dedicated highway lanes that allow *platooning* (multiple vehicles operating close together). Under what circumstances should governments dedicate scarce highway lanes to autonomous vehicles? Is this efficient and fair? What performance and safety standards must a vehicle meet to use those facilities? What user fees should they pay? What regulations and enforcement practices should governments impose?

Although existing publications examine some of these issues, this book is structured to be more comprehensive and systematic. It considers some important but often overlooked issues, such as how new modes can affect household finances, lifestyles, and freedoms. It identifies the modes most suitable for achieving particular goals or for implementing in various conditions. It provides recommendations for maximizing their benefits. It should be of interest to policy makers, practitioners (transportation planners and engineers), investors, and the general public. Although it focuses on North American conditions, much of the analysis is transferable to other regions.

Of course, the world continues to change. This book's evaluation framework and recommendations are designed to be flexible and responsive to new goals and perspectives. For example, because this book was written

BOX 1-1 KEY DEFINITIONS USED IN THIS BOOK

Accessibility is a general term for people's ability to obtain desired goods and reach activities. Mobility (see below) affects accessibility, as do transport network connectivity, land use patterns, user information, and affordability. The term is also sometimes used in reference to universal design (see below).

Active (also called nonmotorized or human-powered) travel includes walking, bicycling, and variants such as wheelchairs and handcarts.

Affordability refers to an activity's financial burden, particularly on lower-income households. North American households spend about 20 percent of their budgets on motor vehicles, including residential parking costs, which many experts consider unaffordable. A more reasonable target is that lower-income households should be able to spend less than 10 percent of their incomes to meet their basic mobility and accessibility needs.

Automobile dependency refers to areas where a combination of abundant road and parking supply and dispersed development patterns make automobile travel convenient and common, but non-auto travel difficult, inefficient, and dangerous. Sprawled development patterns contribute to automobile dependency.

Barrier effect refers to the incremental delay, discomfort, and risk that wider roads and increased motor vehicle traffic speeds and volumes impose on pedestrians and bicyclists.

Community refers to people who live, work, or visit an area, which can be nearly any scale, from a neighborhood to a region or a country.

External costs refers to negative impacts that an activity imposes on other people, such as traffic congestion, barrier effect, crash risk, pollution, or additional infrastructure subsidy needs.

Mobility refers to physical travel, particularly vehicle travel.

Multimodal refers to a transportation system or area where it is easy and common to use diverse mobility options, typically including walking, bicycling, micro modes, taxi/ridehailing, public transportation (buses, trains, ferries, aviation, etc.), and private automobiles, plus New Mobilities such as telework and air taxis.

Public realm refers to public spaces where people interact, such as sidewalks, paths, roadways, public parks, and public buildings.

Resource-efficient travel refers to modes or activities that require less energy and materials, travel, and storage space and less-expensive infrastructure

Smart Growth refers to development policies that create compact, multi-modal communities.

Transportation demand management (TDM) refers to various policies and programs that encourage travelers to use the most efficient mode for each trip.

Universal design refers to transportation facilities, vehicles, and services that accommodate diverse users, including people with mobility impairments, baggage, or other special needs.

during the COVID-19 pandemic, it considers how New Mobilities affect contagion risk, and because of growing social equity concerns, it explores how various modes and policies affect physically, economically, and socially disadvantaged groups. You can add new goals and perspectives that may be important in your community.

Chapter 2

The Arc of
Transportation History

This chapter examines how previous transportation innovations affected people and communities, as well as their resulting economic, social, and environmental impacts.[1]

Transportation innovations transformed society in the past and will surely do so in the future. In ancient times, travel was mostly by foot, so most people seldom ventured beyond their local communities, and imported goods were costly and rare. Over time, new travel modes—wagons, boats, ships, trains, automobiles, and aircraft—expanded where we could go and the goods we could obtain, improving our lives in many ways. Figure 2-1 indicates when new modes became widely available and their typical travel speeds.

To understand how these innovations affect travel activity it is useful to consider two key budgets: time and money. Most people spend sixty to eighty daily minutes and 16 to 20 percent of their household budgets on personal travel.[2] As a result, if travel becomes faster or cheaper we tend to travel further—for example, accepting a longer commute or choosing more distant shopping and holiday destinations. This additional vehicle travel is called *generated traffic* or *induced travel*.[3]

Let's see how transportation innovations affected travel activity during the last 120 years.

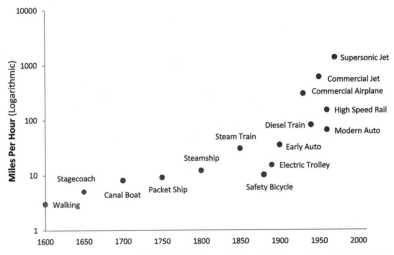

Figure 2-1 New Modes' Initial Availability and Typical Operating Speeds. New transportation modes significantly increased potential travel speeds. Speeds are indicated on a logarithmic scale, so small increases in height indicate large increases in speed. (Various sources including Wikipedia and other encyclopedia articles.)

Roadway Travel

Before 1900, people mainly traveled by foot, with occasional bicycle, train, and boat trips. As motor vehicles developed, travel speeds increased and costs declined. The Ford Model T, the first mass-produced car, had a forty-five-mile-per-hour top speed, but few roads were paved so traffic speeds were usually lower. Its price declined from $850 when it was first released in 1908 to less than $300 in 1920, equivalent to a reduction from $22,000 to $5,000 in current dollars.[4] Over time, automobiles became faster, more convenient, and more comfortable, with features such as automatic transmissions, air conditioning, and sound systems. Roadways also improved. The US Interstate Highway system, constructed between 1956 and 1992, created a network of high-speed highways, and other roads also improved to allow faster traffic. This further increased vehicle travel speeds and reduced their operating costs, which significantly expanded the distances that motorists could travel within their time and money budgets.

The factors that increased traffic speeds eventually reached their practical limits. Starting in the 1970s many communities experienced highway "revolts," which stopped many planned urban freeway projects.[5] Many communities now embrace complete streets policies,[6] road diets,[7] and

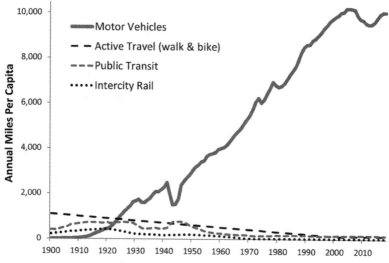

Figure 2-2   Travel Trends: Estimated Annual Passenger-Miles by Mode. Before 1900 people traveled primarily by walking, with occasional bicycle and rail trips. Per capita motor vehicle travel grew steadily during the twentieth century and peaked about 2000. (FHWA [various years]. *Highway Statistics.* Federal Highway Administration, www.fhwa.dot.gov/policyinformation/statistics.cfm. Assumes that in 1900 an average person walked approximately 60 daily minutes at three miles per hour. Current walking and bicycling travel data from John Pucher et al. [2011]. "TABLE 1—Daily and Annual Walking and Cycling Trips, Duration, and Distance, Walking and Cycling in the United States, 2001–2009." *American Journal of Public Health.* Vol. 101, https://doi.org/10.2105/AJPH.2010.300067. Public transit travel data from APTA [2020]. "Appendix A," *Transit Fact Book.* American Public Transportation Association, www.apta.com/wp-content/uploads/APTA-2020 -Fact-Book.pdf. Rail travel data from FRED [2012]. *Railroad Passengers Carried One Mile, All Railroads for United States.* Federal Reserve Bank of St. Louis, https: //fred.stlouisfed.org/series/A0310FUSA251NNBR, and US Census Table Q 44-72, "Railroad Mileage, Equipment, and Passenger Traffic and Revenue: 1890 to 1957." www2.census.gov/library/publications/1960/compendia/hist_stats _colonial-1957/hist_stats_colonial-1957-chQ.pdf. Recent rail passenger data from BLS [2018]. *U.S. Passenger-Miles,* Table 1-40. Bureau of Transportation Statistics, www.bts.gov/content/us-passenger-miles. Due to data gaps and inconsistencies, some early estimates are extrapolated.)

highway removals[8] that reduce traffic speeds. As a result, vehicle travel speeds are declining in many areas.

Figure 2-2 shows changes in per capita travel by various modes during the last 120 years. Walking and bicycling declined from approximately three daily miles in 1900 to one-third of a mile in 2000. Rail and public

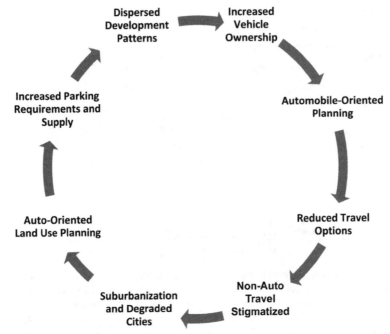

Figure 2-3 Cycle of Automobile Dependency. Many common planning practices contributed to this cycle of automobile dependency and sprawl, which creates communities where it is difficult to get around without a personal automobile. (Todd Litman [2014]. *Analysis of Public Policies That Unintentionally Encourage and Subsidize Urban Sprawl,* commissioned by LSE Cities for the Global Commission on the Economy and Climate, https://urbantransitions.global/wp-content /uploads/2019/09/public-policies-encourage-sprawl-nce-report.pdf.)

transit passenger-miles peaked early during the first half of the twentieth century. Motor vehicle travel grew steadily, from virtually zero in 1900 to approximately ten thousand annual miles per capita in 2000. Overall, per capita mobility increased approximately tenfold during the twentieth century.

For most of the last century, transportation planning favored faster modes over slower modes, and therefore automobile travel over walking, bicycling, and public transit. This created a self-reinforcing cycle of *automobile dependency,* as illustrated in Figure 2-3.[9]

This cycle increased the amount of mobility needed to access services and activities and created communities where it is difficult to get around without driving.[10] Automobile dependency significantly increases vehicle ownership rates, the distances people drive, and the money households must spend on transportation.[11] In recent years, new planning movements, called *New Urbanism*, *Smart Growth*, and *Transit-Oriented Development*, are starting to reverse these trends. Most jurisdictions are now improving walking and bicycling conditions, expanding public transit services, implementing transportation demand management policies, and supporting more compact development.[12]

The COVID-19 pandemic has had mixed impacts on these reforms. It increases contagion concerns and financial stresses. It is likely to increase demand for active travel, micromobilities, and telework; reduce demand and operating efficiencies of public transportation and air travel; and have mixed impacts on private automobile and ridehailing services.[13]

Long-Distance Travel

During the last century, transportation innovations also increased long-distance travel speed and affordability. In 1900, a London to New York steamship trip took about seven *days* and cost about $100 for steerage, equivalent to about $2,500 in current dollars.[14] A London to New York flight now requires about seven *hours*, and costs about $500 for economy class, indicating that during the twentieth century, long-distance travel times declined about 95 percent and prices declined about 80 percent. These cost reductions increased long-distance travel, migration, and trade by orders of magnitude.[15]

Freight Transport

Transportation innovations also improved freight transport speed and affordability. At the start of the twentieth century, freight was transported by horse-drawn wagons, railroads, and steamships. Improved railroads, ships, trucks, and airplanes, plus logistical improvements such as containerization and automation, significantly increased shipping speeds and reduced costs. As a result, freight volumes also grew by orders of magnitude.[16]

Costs

This increased mobility that occured during the last century increased various economic, social, and environmental costs.

User Costs

When walking was the primary travel mode, the largest travel expense was shoe leather. Horse, carriage, boat, and train travel were too expensive for most people's personal travel. Between 1880 and 1900 many cities developed trolley networks, and safety bicycles became affordable in the 1890s, but most people continued to walk for most trips.[17] A 1901 survey of "workingmen's families'" household expenditures had no category for transportation (Figure 2-4), indicating that mobility was an insignificant cost for most moderate-income families.

During the twentieth century, vehicle operation became cheaper as inflation-adjusted fuel prices declined and fuel economy improved, but these savings were offset by rising vehicle ownership costs and increased

AVERAGE EXPENDITURE OF 2,567 WORKINGMEN'S FAMILIES FOR EACH OF THE PRINCIPAL ITEMS ENTERING INTO COST OF LIVING, AND PER CENT OF AVERAGE TOTAL EXPENDITURE, 1901.

Items of expenditure.	Expenditure based on all families.	
	Average.	Per cent of total expenditure.
Food	$326.90	42.54
Rent	99.49	12.95
Mortgage:		
Principal	a 8.15	1.06
Interest	b 3.98	.52
Fuel	32.23	4.19
Lighting	8.15	1.06
Clothing:		
Husband	33.73	4.39
Wife	26.03	3.39
Children	48.08	6.26
Taxes	5.79	.75
Insurance:		
Property	1.53	.20
Life	19.44	2.53
Organizations:		
Labor	3.87	.50
Other	5.18	.67
Religious purposes	7.62	.99
Charity	2.39	.31
Furniture and utensils	26.31	3.42
Books and newspapers	8.35	1.09
Amusements and vacation	12.28	1.60
Intoxicating liquors	12.44	1.62
Tobacco	10.93	1.42
Sickness and death	20.54	2.67
Other purposes	45.13	5.87
Total	768.54	100.00

Figure 2-4 **Workingmen's Families' Household Expenditures in 1901.** This 1901 household expenditure survey had no category for transportation, indicating that prior to the automobile age, transportation expenses were insignificant for most families. (Dept. of Commerce and Labor [1907]. *Bulletin of the United States Bureau of Labor.* Vol. XV, No. 71, p. 195, https://fraser.stlouisfed.org/title/3943 /item/477634/toc/504444?start_page=180.)

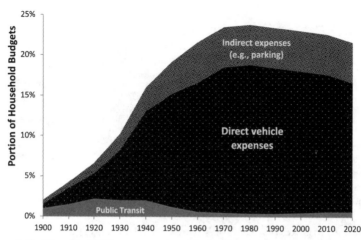

Figure 2-5 Household Transportation Expenditures. Household transportation expenses increased significantly as motor vehicle travel grew. (Based on Bureau of the Census [1908]; Johnson, Rogers, and Tan [2001]; and BLS [various years]. Vehicle and parking expenses for 1900 reflect the portion of households that had horses and carriages for personal use. Indirect costs assume 15 percent of housing expenditures are devoted to residential parking and property taxes spent on local roads.)

vehicle travel, so the portion of household budgets devoted to transportation grew substantially.[18] Most households now spend 16 to 18 percent of their budgets on vehicle expenses,[19] plus 3 to 6 percent on indirect vehicle costs such as residential parking and local taxes devoted to roadways.[20] Figure 2-5 illustrates the portion of household budgets devoted to transportation during the last 120 years.

These costs offset many benefits of increased mobility. A typical automobile commuter spends fifty-two minutes driving to work,[21] plus about ninety-six minutes (20 percent of their workday) earning money to pay vehicle expenses, so their *effective speed* (travel distance divided by time spent traveling and earning money to pay expenses) is often slower than bicycling and transit travel,[22] as illustrated in Figure 2-6.[23] Effective speeds are particularly slow for lower-wage workers, who often spend more time earning money to pay for their vehicles than they do using them. Vehicle costs are much higher in North America than in peer countries. For example, Europeans devote about 11 percent of their household budgets to transportation,[24] compared with more than 17 percent in the United States.[25]

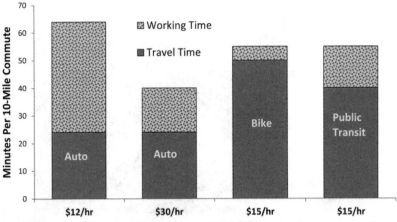

Figure 2-6 Minutes per Mile for Various Travelers. This figure shows effective speed, the time spent traveling and earning money to pay travel expenses for various commuters. Measured this way, bicycling and transit are often faster than driving. (Assumes auto commuters average 25 mph. $12/hr auto commuters spend $4,000 and drive 5,000 annual miles. $30/hr auto commuters spend $6,000 and drive 10,000 annual miles. Bicycle commuters average 12 mph, spend $200 and ride 2,000 annual miles. Transit commuters average 15 mph, spend $600 and travel 2,000 annual miles.)

Public Infrastructure Costs

When somebody purchases a motor vehicle, they expect governments to provide roads and businesses to provide parking for their use. People often assume that these costs are paid through user fees, such as fuel taxes, but in fact, they are largely borne indirectly through general taxes and higher prices for housing and other goods, which consumers pay regardless of how they travel, causing people who drive less than average to subsidize the infrastructure costs of their neighbors who drive more than average. For example, in 2016, governments spent $219 billion on roadways in the United States, of which only $111 billion was funded by user fees.[26] These expenditures average $815 per vehicle, of which approximately $400 can be considered a subsidy.

Similarly, typical North American communities have three to eight government-mandated off-street parking spaces per motor vehicle, with lower rates in urban areas where parking facilities can be shared, and higher rates in suburban and rural areas where each destination must supply all of its own parking.[27] These facilities are expensive. Construction costs average $2,000 to $10,000 per space in surface lots and $20,000 to $60,000 in structures.[28] Considering land, construction, and operating expenses,

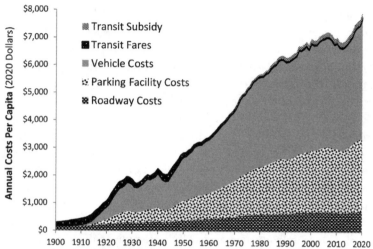

Figure 2-7 Vehicle and Infrastructure Costs, Inflation-Adjusted Dollars. As automobile ownership grew, vehicle and infrastructure costs all increased significantly. (Roadway costs are estimated to average $731 per year in 2020, based on extrapolations from FHWA Highway Statistics reports. Parking costs assumes that there were two off-street spaces per vehicle in 1900, which increased to four by 2000, with $750 average annualized cost. Vehicle costs assumes $4,707 average costs per vehicle-year, based on the US Bureau of Labor Statistics 2018 Consumer Expenditure Survey. Assumes that transit fares average thirty cents per passenger-mile. Transit costs and subsidies are based on APTA *Transit Facts* reports from various years.)

total annualized costs range from approximately $500 for a parking space in a surface lot on inexpensive land up to $3,000 for a structured parking space in a prime location.[29] This typically totals $2,500 to $4,000 in annual parking costs per vehicle, most of which is borne indirectly, representing a large subsidy for automobiles.

Of course, other modes also require public infrastructure: pedestrians use sidewalks, bicyclists use paths, and buses use roads, but automobiles need far more costly facilities due to their greater size, weight, speed, and annual mileage.[30] Figure 2-7 shows total inflation-adjusted vehicle and infrastructure costs, measured per capita.

Health and Environmental Impacts

Motor vehicle travel imposes health and environmental costs including traffic crashes, sedentary living (reduced physical activity and fitness), harmful pollutants, and habitat displacement. Automobile-oriented planning tends to reduce active travel (walking and bicycling), and therefore public fitness and health.[31] Physical inactivity increases the chance of obesity, cardiovascular disease, diabetes, and some forms of cancer. Although many factors affect physical fitness and obesity rates, numerous studies find that these problems tend to increase with more driving and sprawl.[32] This helps explain why residents of sprawled, automobile-dependent areas have more chronic diseases and worse health outcomes than in more compact, multimodal communities,[33] and why residents in the United States have shorter life spans than in most peer countries where people drive less and rely more on walking, bicycling, and public transit.[34]

Motor vehicles emit harmful air pollutants and noise.[35] Although control technologies reduced per-mile emission rates, this has been offset by increased vehicle mileage, so vehicle emissions continue to cause significant health and environmental damages.[36] Recent studies show that disease and death rates tend to increase with proximity to busy highways, indicating that vehicle emissions continue to impose significant health damages.[37] According to one major study, motor vehicles are the single largest cause of US air pollution deaths, resulting in an estimated fifty-three thousand annual fatalities.[38] Motor vehicles also produce about a third of total climate change emissions, the largest single source.[39]

Automobile-oriented planning also threatens the environment by increasing impervious surface (i.e., pavement) for roads and parking facilities.[40] This reduces groundwater recharge, increases flooding and stormwater management costs, increases heat island effects (high ambient temperatures in urban conditions), displaces greenspace, and disrupts habitat.[41]

Opportunity and Equity

The quality of transportation options affects non-drivers' ability to access important services and activities and therefore their economic and social opportunities.[42] New Transportation innovations help disadvantaged people in some ways but harm them in others. For example, *universal design* standards and public transit services improve mobility for people with impairments, but these do not offset the many ways that automobile dependency and sprawl reduce overall accessibility for people who cannot drive.

Wider roads and increased vehicle traffic degrade walking and bicycling conditions. Until the 1920s, it was common and legal to walk through city streets, as you can see in period films such as *A Trip Down Market Street, 1906*[43] and *A Ride Through Barcelona 101 Years Ago*.[44] This mixed traffic forced motorists to drive cautiously. The automobile industry shifted the safety responsibility to pedestrians through campaigns to ridicule and outlaw "jaywalking" (a pejorative term for unsophisticated behavior), forcing pedestrians to yield to automobiles.[45]

Before 1960 the US transit industry earned a healthy profit, but revenues subsequently declined due to a combination of falling ridership, increased traffic congestion, and sprawled development patterns that reduced operating efficiencies.[46] As a result, North Americans have far less transit service than in the past and in most other countries.[47]

The combination of degraded walking and bicycling conditions, reduced transit service, and more dispersed development reduces accessibility for people who cannot drive. This forces non-drivers to travel less, endure unpleasant and dangerous conditions, or depend on drivers for rides. Overall, non-drivers have less independent mobility now than they would have had a century ago.

In addition, motor vehicle traffic imposes external costs on disadvantaged groups. Urban highways displaced many urban neighborhoods or degraded them with increased traffic, noise, pollution, and pavement.[48] African American, Latinx, and Asian communities were particularly vulnerable.[49] The root of the conflict were the common assumptions that (1) faster is better than slower, so (2) automobiles are better than slower modes, so (3) everybody aspires to an automobile-oriented lifestyle, so (4) suburbs are better than cities, so (5) highways to accommodate suburban commuters should replace "blighted" urban neighborhoods, and (6) abundant federal and state funding made highway projects financially attractive, so (7) everybody wins with expanded urban roadways. You could call this the "myth of universal benefits." The harms that automobile-oriented planning caused to vulnerable communities were ignored.

This myth was eventually busted. Public opposition to urban highways resulted in reforms, including more community involvement in planning, and more flexible funding that allows some highway dollars to be "reprogrammed" to non-auto modes.[50] Transportation professionals increasingly recognize that automobile-oriented planning is unfair and inefficient.[51] This results in increasing support for more multimodal planning, particularly in growing cities and lower-income communities.[52]

Will Past Trends Continue?

Many demographic, economic, and technical trends contributed to the immense growth in mobility during the last century. These included population, employment, and income growth; increased travel speeds and reduced travel costs; more sprawled development; and reduced non-auto travel options. Many of these trends are likely to change in the twenty-first century, as summarized in Table 2-1. This suggests that the steady growth in motor vehicle travel that occurred during the last century is unlikely to continue into the future.

Conclusions and Implications

This review of transportation history can help guide future transportation planning. Let's summarize some key insights that apply to New Mobilities.

First, the last 120 years was a period of tremendous change in how and how much people travel. Before 1900 automobiles and aviation hardly existed; by 2000 they were dominant travel modes. Because of faster speeds and lower unit costs we now travel about ten times farther than in 1900. This huge increase in mobility transformed our lives and communities in countless ways. At the start of the twentieth century, most people worked, shopped, and played within their neighborhood; by the end of the century it was normal to drive hundreds of miles per week to destinations scattered throughout a region and to fly thousands of miles for holidays. The world shrank!

Second, although increased mobility provided significant benefits, it also imposed large economic, social, and environmental costs. In 1900, a typical working-class family had negligible transportation expenses. By the end of the century, most households spent more than 20 percent of their budgets on motor vehicles and the roads and parking facilities they require. A typical automobile commuter spends more than two hours each workday driving and earning money to pay for their car. Increasing automobile travel also increased public infrastructure costs, traffic crashes, health problems, environmental damages, and community degradation. Walking, bicycling, and public transit are often more cost effective than driving overall, considering all benefits and costs, but automobile-oriented planning made these modes inconvenient to use. These impacts are particularly harmful to people who cannot drive or have low incomes, and so are inequitable.

Third, high levels of mobility do not necessarily reflect consumer preferences. For the last century, many public policies favored motor vehicles over other modes, and sprawl over compact development. This forces many households to own more vehicles, drive more, and spend more

Table 2-1 Factors Affecting Travel: Past and Future Trends. Many factors that contributed to past mobility growth are unlikely to continue into the twenty-first century.

Factor	Twentieth Century	Twenty-First Century
Travel speed	Travel speeds increased significantly, due to vehicle and road improvements, but peaked during the 1970s.	Speeds are unlikely to increase on most roads, and may decline in many areas due to more congestion, plus safety and environmental goals.
User travel costs	Per-mile vehicle operating costs declined, although total annual costs increased.	Electric vehicles may reduce vehicle operating costs, but most user costs are unlikely to decline.
Travel options	Non-auto modes declined.	Multimodal planning is improving non-auto modes.
Technologies	New technologies made driving more convenient and comfortable.	New technologies are improving many travel options, including non-auto modes.
Demographics and incomes	Large population, employment, and income growth.	Slower population growth, declining workforce participation, and stagnant incomes.
Consumer preferences	Automobile and suburban homes were major status goods.	Many consumers prefer non-auto travel and living in compact, walkable neighborhoods due to growing affordability, health, and environmental concerns.
Land use development	Significant urban expansion (sprawl).	Many urban regions have reached expansion limits and encourage more compact development.
Planning goals	Planning favored automobile travel and sprawl.	Many jurisdictions have vehicle travel reduction targets and so are implementing transportation demand management incentives and Smart Growth policies.

money on transportation than they would choose given better options and incentives.

Fourth, mobility growth is unlikely to continue. Vehicle traffic speeds peaked about 1970 and subsequently declined due to congestion, safety, and environmental concerns. Air travel speeds declined after 2000 due to new security and environmental requirements. Most communities are now implementing more multimodal planning and creating more walkable neighborhoods. Travel *could* be faster if we were willing to bear higher financial, safety, and environmental costs, but there is little public support. Few citizens demand, "Raise my taxes to finance roadway expansions and supersonic jets."

This has important implications for evaluating emerging transportation technologies and services. In the past, transportation innovations were evaluated based primarily on their ability to increase travel speed. We must now give equal consideration to other community goals. The next chapter explores how to apply these insights to New Mobility planning.

Chapter 3

The Context of Transportation Planning

Should transportation planning be *clever* or *wise*? In the past, clever technologies greatly increased mobility, which expanded our world and increased productivity. However, these innovations also increased costs that offset many of their benefits and made some people worse off overall. This has important implications for New Mobility planning. With wiser planning, we can maximize the benefits of these innovations and ensure that they support broader community goals.

Wiser planning will require changing the way we think about problems and solutions.

A New Planning Paradigm

Let's play a simple word-association game.

If I ask you to list *transportation problems*, what springs to mind? Do you focus on conventional problems, such as traffic and parking congestion, crashes, and pollution? What about emerging problems such as unaffordability, inequity, inadequate public fitness, contagion risks, and sprawl costs?

If I asked you to list your preferred *transportation improvements*, what springs to mind? Do you focus on conventional solutions such as roadway expansions, low-emission vehicle incentives, and transit service expansions? What about innovative solutions such as bike- and carsharing services, smartphone navigation and payment apps, autonomous vehicles,

Table 3-1 Comparing the Old and New Transportation Planning Paradigms[i].
The old planning paradigm favored automobile-oriented transportation improvements. The new paradigm considers a wider range of objectives, impacts, and solutions.

	Old Paradigm	New Paradigm
Definition of *Transportation*	*Mobility* (physical travel), particularly automobile travel.	*Accessibility* (people's overall ability to obtain services and participate in activities).
Planning goals	Reduce traffic congestion, vehicle operating costs and per-mile crash rates.	Reduce traffic and parking congestion, consumer savings and affordability, social equity goals (improved opportunity for disadvantaged people), traffic safety, public fitness and health, energy conservation, pollution reductions, more accessible development.
Modes considered	Mainly automobile. Considers other modes inefficient and unimportant.	Multimodal: walking, cycling, public transport, automobile, shared vehicles, telework, and delivery services.
Favored transport improvements	Roadway capacity expansion.	Improve mobility options (walking, cycling, public transit, etc.) and efficiently manage travel demands.
Performance indicators	Vehicle traffic speeds, roadway level-of-service (LOS), distance-based crash and emission rates.	Quality of accessibility for various groups. Multimodal LOS. Various economic, social, and environmental impacts.

[i] Todd Litman (2013). "The New Transportation Planning Paradigm." *ITE Journal*, 83(6), pp. 20–28, www.vtpi.org/paradigm.pdf.

mobility prioritization, and Smart Growth development policies to create more accessible neighborhoods?

Your responses reflect your *paradigm*—that is, how you define problems and evaluate solutions. Transportation practitioners and the organizations they work in are undergoing a *paradigm shift*, a change in how we think about these problems and solutions.[1] Table 3-1 compares the old and new paradigms.

The old paradigm assumed that our primary goal is to maximize vehicle travel speeds and therefore the distances that people can travel within their limited travel time budgets. It evaluated transportation system performance based on motor vehicle travel conditions, using indicators such as roadway level-of-service (LOS) and congestion delay.[2] The new paradigm considers a wider range of goals and impacts. It recognizes that mobility is seldom an end in itself, since the ultimate goal of most travel is to access desired services and activities.[3] It therefore evaluates transportation system performance using multifaceted accessibility indicators that include mobility, system connectivity, geographic proximity, and affordability.[4] This expands the range of solutions that can be applied to transportation problems. For example, it recognizes the increased accessibility provided by improvements to active modes (walking and bicycling) and public transit services, better connections between modes, more compact development that increases proximity between activities, and mobility substitutes such as telework and delivery services.

The new paradigm often turns planning priorities on their head. Think about your community's ugliest road, perhaps a six-lane arterial lined with gas stations and big-box stores surrounded by acres of parking and capped with big, brash signs designed to catch motorists' attention. It is optimized for cars, not people. The old paradigm considers such roads ideal due to their high design speeds and abundant traffic and parking capacity. They receive a high level-of-service rating. Now, think about your favorite road, perhaps a pedestrian-oriented shopping street, or a tree-lined boulevard. It has wide sidewalks and low traffic speeds, and during busy periods motorists must park a few blocks away, but that's not a problem because the walk is pleasant. The old paradigm would give it a low rating due to inadequate traffic and parking capacity, and so justifies road and parking expansions to improve automobile access. In contrast, the new paradigm gives such streets a high rating because they offer excellent multimodal accessibility and accommodate diverse users and uses.[5] Applying the new paradigm is like wearing corrective glasses; it puts our complex world into clearer focus.

Let's consider another example. Imagine that roads around a local school are increasingly congested due to more students arriving by car. The old planning paradigm defines the problem as insufficient road capacity. Since most jurisdictions have dedicated roadway budgets, local officials can easily solve this problem with roadway expansion projects, and since most public officials are themselves busy motorists, their personal experiences validate this solution. However, wider roads with increased vehicle

Table 3-2 Benefits of Multimodalism[i]. Multimodal transportation provides many types of benefits.

Economic	Social	Environmental
• Consumer savings and affordability (savings to lower-income households). • Road and parking facility cost savings. • Improved economic opportunity for non-drivers. • More local economic development.	• Reduced chauffeuring burdens. • More independent mobility for non-drivers. • Traffic safety. • Increased public fitness and health.	• Reduced air pollution. • Reduced traffic noise. • Resource conservation. • Less sprawled development. • Reduced impervious surface and habitat preservation.

[i] Susan Handy (2020). *What California Gains from Reducing Car Dependence.* National Center for Sustainable Transportation, https://escholarship.org/uc/item/0hk0h610.

traffic make active travel unpleasant and dangerous, causing even more parents to drive their children, which further exacerbates the problem. This creates a self-reinforcing cycle of increased driving, expanded roads, and less affordable travel options. This cycle harms many people, including children who lose opportunities for exercise and independence, parents who must spend more time and money chauffeuring, and nearby residents who suffer more traffic risk, noise, and pollution.

The new paradigm considers other perspectives and solutions. It defines the problem as too little road capacity *or* too much driving. It recognizes additional costs caused by increased motor vehicle traffic and additional benefits provided by a more diverse and efficient transportation system. It therefore supports active transportation and public transit improvements, traffic calming, and TDM incentives that encourage school students, parents, and staff to use efficient modes. The new paradigm does not forbid people from driving children to school; there are often legitimate reasons to do so. However, it strives to ensure that anybody who wants to use a more resource-efficient mode can easily do so. This justifies spending at least as much to accommodate a pedestrian or bicycle trip as would be spent to accommodate more automobile trips, and perhaps more due to the additional benefits provided by active travel.

The new paradigm recognizes that many people cannot, should not, or prefer not to drive. This justifies more multimodal planning, so each mode can play its appropriate role in a diverse and efficient transport system.

Although few people want to forgo driving completely, surveys indicate that many want to drive less, rely more on other modes, live in more multimodal neighborhoods, and spend less time and money on transportation.[6] The new paradigm responds to these demands. This is good news, because more multimodal transportation provides many benefits, as summarized in Table 3-2.

This has important implications for New Mobility planning. The old paradigm undervalued slower but affordable and resource-efficient modes. The new paradigm recognizes more of their benefits and therefore gives those modes more support.

Transportation Planning Principles

In the next decades, governments will need to make countless decisions concerning New Mobilities, including some that involve complex trade-offs between diverse goals and perspectives. This could seem overwhelming, but fortunately there is practical guidance for such decisions. This section describes principles for efficient and equitable transportation planning.

Comprehensive Analysis: Consider Often Overlooked Goals and Impacts

To be efficient and fair, planning must consider all significant goals and impacts.[7] As described previously, conventional planning tends to evaluate transportation system performance based primarily on motor vehicle traffic conditions. Other impacts tend to be overlooked, as indicated in Table 3-3.

These often-overlooked impacts are important. For example, the National Household Travel Survey asked respondents to prioritize six transportation planning issues. The "price of travel" (i.e., affordability) received the highest rank, much higher than traffic congestion or safety, as shown in Figure 3-1. However, conventional transportation planning gives little consideration to affordability. It sometimes considers vehicle operating costs but ignores other vehicle costs, and so undervalues improvements

Table 3-3 Scope of Impacts Considered[i]. Conventional transportation planning tends to focus on a limited set of impacts.

Usually Considered	Often Overlooked
• Traffic speed and congestion delays • Vehicle operating costs (fuel, tolls, tire wear) • Per-mile crash risk • Public infrastructure costs	• User comfort and convenience (e.g., by transit passenger) • Affordability (transportation costs relative to incomes) • Parking congestion and facility costs • Mobility for non-drivers • Social equity impacts • Per capita crash risk • Public fitness and health • Barrier effect (delay to pedestrians and cyclists) • Environmental impacts • Local economic development • Induced vehicle travel and downstream traffic impacts • Strategic land use objectives (compact development)

[i] Todd Litman (2018). *Toward More Comprehensive and Multi-modal Transport Evaluation.* Victoria Transport Policy Institute, www.vtpi.org/comp_evaluation.pdf.

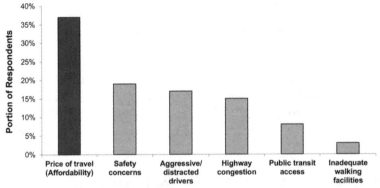

Figure 3-1 Transportation Issues Ratings. National Household Travel Survey respondents ranked "price of travel" (affordability) as the most important of six transport issues. Conventional transportation analysis generally ignores this concern. (Jeremy Mattson [2012]. *Travel Behavior and Mobility of Transportation-Disadvantaged Populations: Evidence from the National Household Travel Survey.* Upper Great Plains Transportation Institute, www.ugpti.org/pubs/pdf/DP258.pdf.)

to affordable modes and the transportation savings provided by compact development that reduces travel distances.

Respond to Diverse Consumer Demands

Consumer sovereignty means that markets (in this case, a transportation system is considered a market for mobility) respond to consumer demands. Optimal transportation planning therefore asks, "What do travelers want?" and "What are communities' goals?" For example, if more travelers want to walk and bicycle, responsive planning improves sidewalks, crosswalks, and bicycle facilities. Similarly, if a community has goals to increase affordability, social equity, public health, or environmental quality, transportation planning should favor modes that support those goals.

Surveys indicate significant demand for affordable and healthy mobility. The National Association of Realtors 2017 *National Community and Transportation Preference Survey* found that 80 percent of respondents enjoy walking, 53 percent enjoy bicycling, 38 percent enjoy public transit, 40 percent want to bicycle more than they currently do, and 59 percent report that they drive more than they want. It found that more than half of respondents would prefer living in multifamily housing located in a walkable neighborhood over a single-family house located in a sprawled, automobile-dependent area. Younger people are much more likely to prefer walking, bicycling, public transit, and walkable neighborhoods, suggesting that the demand for accessible neighborhoods will increase in the future. Conventional planning tends to overlook and undervalue these preferences; it continues to spend far more money on automobile facilities, directly and through parking facility mandates, than on other modes. To be more efficient and fair, our planning practices must respond to this growing demand for non-auto modes, and for housing in multimodal neighborhoods.

Price Services Efficiently

A basic economic principle is that prices (what consumers pay for a good) should reflect the marginal costs of producing that good, unless subsidies are specifically justified. As much as possible, travelers should pay for the facilities they use and compensate for any external costs they impose; in other words, users should "get what they pay for and pay for what they get."

Several studies have developed estimates of the costs and benefits of various modes, including the UK Department for Transport's *Transport Analysis Guidance* website,[8] the European Union's *Handbook on External Costs of Transport*,[9] New Zealand Transport Agency's *Economic Evaluation Manual*,[10] and my report *Transportation Cost and Benefit Analysis*.[11]

These studies indicate that vehicle travel is significantly underpriced. As described in the previous chapter, every year governments in the United States spend more than $800 on roads,[12] and businesses spend thousands of dollars on off-street parking facilities for each automobile.[13] Most of these costs are borne indirectly: your taxes, your home, and most things that you purchase are more expensive to subsidize roads and parking facilities. Motor vehicles impose other external costs, including traffic congestion, crash risk, and pollution damages, plus economic and environmental costs caused by fossil fuel production and sprawl.[14]

In addition, most vehicle costs are fixed; motorists pay about the same amount for vehicle depreciation, financing, registration fees, and insurance premiums regardless of how much they drive. This is another significant form of underpricing. This price structure encourages vehicle owners to drive more in order to get their money's worth from these large expenditures. It is therefore inefficient and unfair. It fails to encourage travelers to use resource-efficient modes, and it forces people who drive less than average to subsidize the costs of their neighbors who drive more than average.

Of course, other modes also use public infrastructure: pedestrians use sidewalks, bicycles use paths and bike parking, and buses use roads, but their annual costs are much lower compared with automobile travel due to their smaller size, lower speeds, and low annual mileage.[15]

Figure 3-2 compares my estimates of the full costs of various modes, measured per passenger-mile. On average, car travel is a little cheaper than bus travel, due to the high costs of providing bus services in lower-density areas where demand is low. However, under urban-peak conditions, buses have lower costs than automobile travel due to higher congestion, parking, crash risk, and pollution costs caused by driving on crowded city roads.

Total annual costs are also affected by the distances people travel. Figure 3-3 compares the estimated annual costs per user, assuming that motorists drive ten thousand annual miles, and travelers dependant on other modes average three thousand annual miles. Because of their high unit costs and high annual mileage, motorists' total costs are generally much higher than those of non-drivers.

Of course, these costs can vary depending on conditions and analysis assumptions, such as the types of vehicles used, geographic factors such as

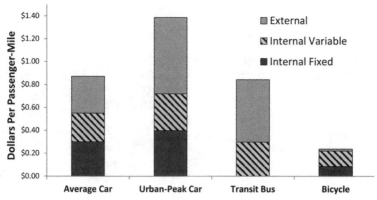

Figure 3-2 Estimated Costs by Mode. This figure compares the costs of various travel modes, measured per passenger-mile. (Todd Litman [2019]. "Transportation Cost Analysis Spreadsheet." Victoria Transport Policy Institute, www.vtpi.org/tca /tca.xls. Excludes "Transport Diversity" and "Land Use Impacts" categories.)

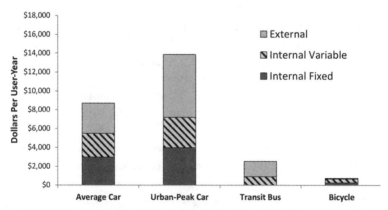

Figure 3-3 Estimated Annual Costs by Mode User. This figure compares the total annual costs of various travel modes, taking into account the greater annual travel by motorists compared with people who depend on other modes. (Litman [2019]. "Transportation Cost Analysis Spreadsheet.")

density and terrain, and the values assigned to human lives and pollution damages. However, virtually all transportation cost studies agree that motor vehicle travel is inefficiently priced and imposes significant external costs.[16] As a result, pricing reforms can increase efficiency and equity and help solve problems.[17] For example, *cost recovery road and parking pricing* (road tolls and parking fees that repay facility costs) typically reduce affected vehicle travel by 10 to 30 percent.[18] Distance-based vehi-

Figure 3-4 Billboard Truck. Billboard trucks drive around on busy roads to attract attention. This is legal but wasteful because it increases traffic congestion, roadway costs, accidents, and pollution. Such vehicle travel would probably not occur if urban streets were efficiently priced, indicating that it is economically inefficient: its costs exceed its benefits. (Photo by author.)

cle registration fees and insurance premiums reduce driving by 10 to 12 percent.[19] *Decongestion pricing* (road tolls that increase with congestion) gives higher-value vehicle travel, such as emergency, freight, and high-occupancy vehicles, priority over lower-value vehicles, such as flexible personal errands and billboard trucks, as illustrated in Figure 3-4.[20]

Billboard trucks are just one of many examples of low-value vehicle travel that results from inefficient pricing. Although some automobile travel has high value and lacks alternatives, most motorists make vehicle trips that could easily shift to more efficient modes, closer destinations, cleaner vehicles, or mobility substitutes, but they lack incentives. Efficient pricing prevents society from spending two dollars to accommodate vehicle travel that users value at only one dollar. It reduces the subsidies from people who drive less than average, and therefore impose lower-than-average costs, to their neighbors who drive more than average, and so impose higher than average costs. Since automobile travel tends to increase with income, efficient pricing tends to be progressive. For example, people with disabilities and low incomes tend to benefit if decongestion pricing reduces bus delays, particularly if a portion of revenues are used to improve public transit services.[21]

Efficient pricing does not reject all subsidies. Transportation subsidies can be justified to provide basic mobility for people with low incomes, to improve efficient modes in order to reduce traffic problems, to take advantage of economies of scale (in which case a small subsidy can provide large benefits), or to stimulate development of a new mode that has strategic value.

Invest for Maximum Efficiently: Apply Least-Cost Planning

Least-cost planning means that resources are allocated to the most cost-effective option, considering all impacts.[22] You might assume that this already occurs, that transportation planners carefully consider all possible transportation improvements, rank them according to cost efficiency, and allocate money to the best. The truth is very different. With current practices, some solutions, such as highway and parking facility expansions, are much easier to plan, approve, and finance than other solutions, such as active and public transport improvements, and TDM programs. As a result, most jurisdictions spend far more to support automobile travel than other modes, even if those alternatives are more affordable, efficient, and beneficial overall. This is a major cause of automobile dependency.[23] These biases could cause underinvestment in New Mobilities that do not fit into existing transportation investment categories, or that provide benefits that are currently undervalued such as affordability, social equity, and public health.

Least-cost planning tends to create more multimodal transportation systems and supports TDM solutions.[24] My research suggests that more multimodal planning and efficient pricing could reduce vehicle travel by 25 to 50 percent, with particularly large reductions in urban-peak vehicle travel, providing large reductions in traffic congestion, crash, and pollution problems.[25] Least-cost planning is likely to support New Mobilities that are resource efficient and provide diverse benefits, such as active modes, public transit innovations, telework, Mobility as a Service, and mobility prioritization.

To support these reforms some jurisdictions have established vehicle travel reduction targets.[26] This encourages decision-makers to apply least-cost planning and implement TDM incentives. For example, California has a target to reduce per capita annual vehicle travel 15 percent by 2050,[27] and Washington State has a target to reduce per capita annual vehicle travel 30 percent by 2035 and 50 percent by 2050.[28] This is sometimes called a shift from LOS to VMT, referring to a change in planning goals from maximizing roadway level-of-service (LOS) to minimizing vehicle miles traveled (VMT).[29] Guides and tools are now available for incorporating these targets into policy and planning decisions.[30]

Examples of Successful Change

There are many good examples of communities that, by improving travel options and providing suitable incentives, have significantly increased transportation system diversity and efficiency. There are good reasons for more communities to follow these examples.

When communities improve mobility options, people drive less. For example, the US Federal Highway Administration's Nonmotorized Transportation Pilot Program, which invested about one hundred dollars per capita in pedestrian and bicycling improvements in four typical communities (Columbia, Missouri; Marin County, California; Minneapolis area, Minnesota; and Sheboygan County, Wisconsin), caused walking trips to increase 23 percent and cycling trips to increase 48 percent, mostly for utilitarian purposes.[31]

In Washington State, a combination of transit service improvements, rideshare incentives, pedestrian and bicycling improvements, and commute trip reduction programs caused automobile mode shares to decline and use of other modes to increase significantly in the Puget Sound region.[32] For trips to downtown Seattle, automobile mode shares declined from 50 percent to 25 percent while transit modes shares increased from 29 percent to 48 percent between 2010 and 2017.[33]

Stanford University in Palo Alto, California, is significantly expanding its facilities to accommodate more students and staff, but this growth was constrained by limited roadway capacity.[34] An agreement with local governments allowed the university to add buildings provided that there was no increase in total vehicle traffic to campus. To achieve this goal the university developed a transportation management plan that includes improved, fare-free transit service, pedestrian and bicycle improvements, a ridesharing program, parking cash-out (non-drivers receive the cash equivalent of parking subsidies provided to motorists), and other incentives. This allowed the campus to add millions of square feet of buildings with minimal planning or environmental review, avoided tens of millions of dollars in road and parking facility costs, reduced traffic congestion and pollution emissions, and improved mobility options for non-drivers. Many campuses around the world are having similar success.[35]

There is significant latent demand for affordable housing in walkable and transit-oriented neighborhoods.[36] In response, many cities are creating fifteen-minute neighborhoods, where residents can reach commonly-used services and activities within a fifteen-minute walk of their homes.[37] For example, the City of Vancouver has a goal of 90 percent of residents living within an easy walk or roll of their daily needs by 2030 and two-thirds of all travel in the city to be by active and public transport modes.[38] Residents of such communities tend to own fewer automobiles, generate 30 to 60 percent less vehicle travel, and rely more on walking, bicycling, and public transit than they would in automobile-dependent, sprawled areas.[39] As a result, they tend to be healthier, safer, and more economically successful and resilient, causing less traffic congestion and pollution.[40] Improving affordable housing options in multimodal neighborhoods can therefore help achieve transportation equity and public health goals.

These and other examples indicate that many people want more multimodal lifestyles, and so will respond favorably to better mobility options and incentives.

Conclusions

The way we think about transportation problems is changing. Until recently, transportation planning focused on automobile improvements, to the detriment of slower, more affordable and resource-efficient modes. A new paradigm considers more impacts and options, including multimodal planning and TDM solutions. This tends to benefit everybody, including motorists, who experience less traffic and parking congestion, lower crash risks, and reduced chauffeuring burdens.

The principles described in this chapter can help guide planning to better respond to consumer demands and community goals. These principles apply to all types of transportation, including emerging modes and services, and so can help guide New Mobility planning.

Chapter 4

A Comprehensive Evaluation Framework

Which New Mobilities are good and which are bad for your community? Under what circumstances should they be mandated, encouraged, regulated, restricted, or forbidden? These are complicated questions. New transportation technologies and services can have many different effects on users and communities. As a result, we need a comprehensive analysis framework that considers diverse impacts and perspectives.

For example, some modes may seem beneficial to affluent travelers but undesirable to lower-income travelers, particularly if they displace more affordable modes or impose external costs, such as congestion, danger, or pollution, on community members. Decision-makers should consider all of these impacts and perspectives when evaluating a transportation policy or program.

Toward More Comprehensive Evaluation

Transportation planning decisions can have many impacts, including some benefits and costs that are generally overlooked or undervalued in conventional analysis. Conventional transportation evaluation methods were developed to answer relatively simple questions, such as whether the costs of a highway improvement will be repaid through travel time and vehicle operating cost savings. That is sufficient for some decisions but is unsuited to comparing different modes or new technologies that have diverse impacts. When people consider a new transportation option they want to know not only how it will affect traffic speeds but also its convenience and comfort, the types of trips and travelers it can serve, its direct and indirect costs, safety and security, how it will impact nonusers, whether it supports or conflicts with a community's strategic goals, and its contagion risk.

For example, although every vehicle trip ends at a parking space, until recently, parking costs, and therefore the parking cost savings of non-auto modes, were ignored in most transportation project evaluations.[1] Similarly, conventional analysis assumed that everybody (at least, everybody who matters) has an automobile that would simply sit unused if travelers shift to modes that don't require parking. In recent years, some professional organizations and government agencies developed more comprehensive analysis frameworks that consider additional impacts, and so are more suited to multimodal planning.[2] For example, the United Kingdom's *Transport Analysis Guidance*,[3] the *Australian Transport Assessment and Planning Guidelines*,[4] New Zealand's *Economic Evaluation Manual*,[5] the European Union's *Guide to Cost-Benefit Analysis of Investment Projects*,[6] and my report *Transportation Cost and Benefit Analysis*[7] provide detailed information on the costs and benefits of various modes of travel, as well as practical guidance for using that information for multimodal analysis.

A little skepticism is appropriate when evaluating new technologies and services. Some New Mobilities are promoted with glamorous images of happy passengers traveling in sleek, fast, clean vehicles, but the reality may be very different. In practice, autonomous taxis, tunnel roads, pneumatic tube transport, and supersonic jets will often be less comfortable than common alternatives, and their door-to-door travel time savings modest. For example, autonomous taxi passengers may find garbage, stains, and odors left by previous occupants; tunnel roads lack views and fresh air; pneumatic tube travel will probably cause many people to be nauseous; and because of its high costs, supersonic jet travel will be cost effective only for travelers who value travel time savings at thousands of dollars per hour. As a result, their user benefits, and therefore their future ridership and revenues, are likely to be smaller, perhaps much smaller, than optimists predict.

Some impacts are important but difficult to measure. For example, social equity is an important community goal, but there are many possible ways to define and measure it.[8] It is generally best to identify specific equity objectives, such as improving *universal design* (transportation facilities and services that accommodate people with impairments and other special needs—for example, facilities and vehicles with features to accommodate wheelchairs and handcarts, and signage suitable for people who lack reading proficiency), increasing *affordability*, improving *mobility options* for disadvantaged groups, and reducing *external costs* (displacement, risk, noise, air pollution) imposed on disadvantaged groups. This analysis should consider indirect, cumulative, and long-term impacts.

Impacts are generally compared with what would otherwise occur (what economists call *ceteris paribus*). What we assume to be the alternative can affect analysis results. For example, carsharing and ridehailing tend to reduce total vehicle travel if they help households reduce their vehicle ownership but can increase total vehicle travel if they substitute for walking, bicycling, and public transit. Electric vehicle benefit analysis depends on the type of vehicle we assume those motorists would otherwise use, and whether we consider the induced vehicle travel that tends to result from their low operating costs.

All too often, transportation policy and planning decisions are evaluated based on incomplete and biased analysis. For example, for the last half century transportation funding was allocated based primarily on how expenditures could increase traffic speeds and reduce congestion, ignoring other impacts and goals.[9] This tended to favor highway expansions and undervalued other modes and TDM solutions. Similarly, environmental studies, such as Project Drawdown, evaluate transportation policies based only on their climate emission reduction impacts. That type of evaluation tends to favor alternative-fueled vehicle incentives while undervaluing vehicle travel reduction strategies that provide a broader range of benefits.[10]

Described differently, more comprehensive analysis helps identify "win-win" transportation solutions—that is, the congestion reduction strategies that also help reduce emissions, improve public health, and achieve social equity goals, called *co-benefits*.[11] This is illustrated in Table 4-1, which compares the range of planning objectives achieved by three transportation policies. Roadway expansions may improve automobile passenger comfort and reduce congestion, at least for a few years until induced travel fills the additional road capacity. More efficient and alternative-fueled vehicles help conserve energy and reduce pollution emissions but provide few other benefits, and by reducing the cost of driving, they tend to induce additional vehicle travel that exacerbates other transportation problems. However, improving resource-efficient modes and implementing TDM incentives that reduce total vehicle travel tends to help achieve a wide range of community goals.

Table 4-1 Comparing Strategies[i]. Some transport improvement strategies help achieve one or two goals. Improving resource-efficient modes, and TDM incentives that reduce total vehicle travel, help achieve many planning objectives, and so can be considered "win-win" solutions.

Community Goals	Roadway Expansion	More Efficient and Alt. Fuel Vehicles	Efficient Modes and TDM Incentives
User convenience and comfort	✓		✓
Congestion reduction	✓		✓
Parking cost savings			✓
Roadway facility costs savings			✓
Consumer costs savings			✓
Reduced traffic accidents			✓
Improved mobility options			✓
Energy conservation		✓	✓
Pollution reductions		✓	✓
Physical fitness and health			✓
Land use objectives			✓

[i] Todd Litman (2020). *Toward More Comprehensive and Multi-Modal Transport Evaluation.* Victoria Transport Policy Institute, www.vtpi.org/comp_evaluation.pdf.

Measuring Impacts

Transportation planning decisions often involve projects costing millions or even billions of dollars, far too large for most people to comprehend. It is important to break these down into more understandable units. Which units are used can affect analysis results.

For example, transportation planning studies sometimes compare the cost effectiveness of infrastructure projects such as highway expansions, new rail lines, and bus lanes. How should such comparisons be structured? Should they compare costs or subsidies per facility-mile, per passenger-mile, or per additional user? Should they consider just the project costs, or total costs per trip, including the costs of vehicles (automobiles, trains, and buses), terminals (parking facilities, train stations, and bus stops), and future operating expenses? Should the analysis disaggregate by user class— for example, compare the costs and benefits by geographic area, income class, or ability?

For most analysis, it is generally best to measure impacts annual per capita, so they are easy to understand and compare. For example, a 2020 study estimated that upgrading all sidewalks in Albuquerque, New Mexico, would cost approximately $54 million.[12] Since most people are unfamiliar with public infrastructure budgets, they would probably consider that expensive. However, that cost could also be described as less than $5 annual per capita, which is tiny compared with what governments spend on roads (about $800 annual per capita), what businesses spend to subsidize parking facilities (more than $2,000 annual per capita), and what households spend on automobiles (about $5,000 annual per capita). Described this way, sidewalk improvements are inexpensive. The cost of improving the sidewalks could easily be recouped if they result in even small reductions in roadway costs or vehicle expenses.

Analysis should be comprehensive, considering all possible impacts and perspectives. Impacts that are unsuited for quantification should be described and, where appropriate, rated or ranked. A framework that uses a mixture of analysis methods is called *multi-criteria evaluation*.

The next section describes how I apply these guidelines to New Mobility planning.

Evaluation Framework

An *evaluation framework* defines the impacts and perspectives considered in an analysis. What follows is the framework I use in this book to evaluate the New Mobilities. It considers various impacts and planning goals. These were selected to be comprehensive without being too technical and to reflect various perspectives, including users, communities, and businesses. It is a multi-criteria framework that incorporates both quantitative and qualitative information—that is, some impacts are measured, and others are ranked or just described. This allows it to consider impacts that are important but unsuited to quantification. For example, it considers how modes are likely to affect social equity, public health, and strategic community goals. You can adjust and expand this framework, as needed, for your own analysis.

This evaluation framework describes, and where appropriate quantifies, the following impacts for each of the twelve New Mobilities.

Current Status

This section discusses a new mode's state of development. Technological development generally follows a predictable cycle, often called an innova-

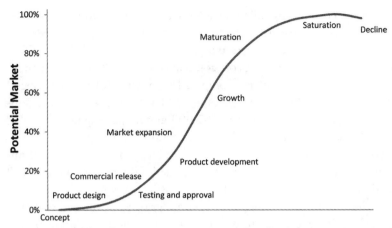

Figure 4-1 Cycle of Innovation. Most new technologies follow a predictable development pattern, often called an innovation S-curve. Some New Mobilities are in the design, testing, and approval stage, while others are already commercially available and in their growth phases.

tion S-curve: an initial concept undergoes design, testing and approval, commercial release, product development, market expansion, growth, maturation, and eventually saturation and decline, as illustrated in Figure 4-1.

Previous vehicle innovations followed this pattern. For example, automatic transmissions first became commercially available in the 1940s but were initially unreliable and expensive. It took until the 1980s for this technology to become reliable and affordable and standard on many new vehicles. In some countries over half of all new vehicles still have manual transmissions. Air bags were introduced in 1973 but were initially an expensive option. They became standard on some models starting in 1988 and mandated by US federal regulation in 1998. Vehicle navigation systems were expensive accessories starting in the 1990s. Their performance improved and prices declined and are now standard in many models.

This indicates that new vehicle technologies typically require one to three decades to mature and saturate the new vehicle market, and since only about 5 percent of vehicles are replaced each year, new vehicle technologies generally require three to six decades to penetrate vehicle fleets unless large numbers of otherwise functional vehicles are scrapped prematurely to accelerate turnover.

User Experience

This section discusses how a new mode is experienced by users, including factors such as convenience and comfort. This affects user benefits and costs, and demand for that mode, that is, the degree that consumers will choose it over alternatives. The user experience of some New Mobilities can be compared with previous conditions. For example, active and public transit improvements can improve the comfort and convenience of walking, bicycling, micro modes, and public transit travel. Others can be compared with their most likely alternatives. For example, the air taxi travel experience can be compared with automobile travel, and the pneumatic tube transport user experience can be compared with commercial air travel.

Travel Impacts

This section discusses how a mode affects travel activity, including whether it is likely to increase or reduce total motor vehicle mileage. New Mobilities can reduce total vehicle travel directly if they substitute for automobile travel, and indirectly if they help households reduce their vehicle ownership or encourage more compact community development. Conversely, New Mobilities that increase the convenience or reduce the costs of automobile travel tend to induce more vehicle-miles of travel.

Benefits and Costs

This analysis describes, and where possible quantifies, the following impacts of each New Mobility.

TRAVEL SPEEDS AND TRAVEL TIME COSTS

This includes changes in travel speeds, usually measured door-to-door, taking into account access and waiting time. It can also include changes in travel time unit costs (dollars per hour) if a mode reduces stress or allows people to be more productive while traveling.

USER COSTS AND AFFORDABILITY

This considers all financial costs of using a mode. Affordability refers to costs relative to incomes, and whether it can provide significant savings to lower-income travelers.

PUBLIC INFRASTRUCTURE COSTS

This includes all incremental costs of public facilities such as paths, roads, terminals, and public transit services, plus government-owned or government-mandated parking facilities.

CONGESTION COSTS

This reflects the amount of road space required per passenger-mile, and therefore the amount of congestion each traveler imposes on other road users. This can also include delays that wider roads and increased vehicle traffic may impose on active and micro modes, called the *barrier effect*.

CRASH RISK

This reflects changes in crash risks caused by a New Mobility, including "external" risks that vehicles impose on other road users.

SOCIAL EQUITY OBJECTIVES

This refers to the impacts that a technology or service can have on the mobility of vulnerable people, such as those who are lower income or have physical disabilities. It can also include any delay, danger, or pollution that a mode imposes on other people, particularly those who are more vulnerable.

RESOURCE CONSUMPTION

This refers to impacts on the consumption of energy and other scarce resources. This is sometimes measured based on life cycle impacts, which include the resources embodied into the production of infrastructure and vehicles, in addition to the vehicle use.

POLLUTION EMISSIONS

This refers to the additional noise and air pollution emitted by a mode, as well as the number of people impacted.

PUBLIC FITNESS AND HEALTH

This includes impacts on the amount of physical activity that people engage in and the likelihood that they will achieve physical fitness targets, such as recommendations that people engage in at least 150 minutes of moderate physical activity each week. Since active travel is the most com-

Table 4-2 Analysis Framework. This table summarizes the factors considered in this evaluation framework and identifies those that are of particular interest to potential users, industry, and the community perspective.

	Potential Users	Industry	Community
Current status	✓	✓	✓
User experience	✓	✓	
Travel impacts	✓		✓
Travel speeds and time costs	✓		✓
User costs and affordability	✓		✓
Public infrastructure costs			✓
Congestion costs imposed on others			✓
Crash risk	✓		✓
Social equity objectives	✓		✓
Resource consumption			✓
Pollution emissions			✓
Public fitness and health	✓		✓
Contagion risk	✓		✓
Effects on strategic planning goals			✓
Roles	✓	✓	✓

mon form of daily exercise, changes in walking and bicycling activity tend to affect overall fitness and health in a community.

DISEASE CONTAGION RISK

This considers the degree that a mode exposes people to infectious diseases. This risk is higher for enclosed rather than unenclosed modes and tends to increase with the number of passengers who occupy a vehicle, the degree of crowding, and the duration of trips.

EFFECTS ON STRATEGIC PLANNING GOALS

This refers to whether a mode helps create more diverse, multimodal transportation systems, helps achieve vehicle travel reduction targets, encourages more compact development patterns, or supports other long-term community goals.

Roles

This section discusses the most appropriate roles that a mode can play in an efficient and equitable transportation system, taking into account factors such as the types of community goals it helps achieve and the types of trips or geographic conditions in which it is most effective and beneficial.

Conclusion

Table 4-2 summarizes the factors considered in this analysis framework and identifies those that are most important from particular perspectives. For example, potential users are particularly interested in the user experience, while a community perspective is particularly interested in how a new mode affects public infrastructure and congestion costs, plus whether it helps achieve social equity objectives and strategic goals.

The next chapter applies this framework to each of the New Mobilities.

Chapter 5

Evaluating the New Mobilities

This chapter systematically evaluates the New Mobilities with regard to various impacts, based on the framework described in chapter 4. This information will be used in the next chapter to rate and compare them with regard to various community goals.

Active Travel and Micromobility

Active (also called *non-motorized* or *human-powered*) *travel* includes walking, bicycling, and variants such as wheelchairs and handcarts. *Micromobilities* are light, low-speed motorized modes such as e-bikes, e-scooters, and motorized skateboards (see Figure 5-1).[1] They often use active mode facilities such as sidewalks, paths, bike lanes, and bicycle parking.

Of course, active modes are not new: walking is the oldest form of mobility, and bicycles have been commercially available since the early 1880s. However, for most of the last century these modes were considered slow and inefficient, and therefore out of date, to be replaced by faster motorized modes where possible. The new planning paradigm recognizes the important and unique roles that active and micro modes can play in an efficient and equitable transportation system, by providing affordable basic mobility, access to motorized modes, healthy exercise, and enjoyment.[2] It also recognizes the importance of an attractive public realm, with appealing and vibrant public streets that are comfortable for walking, playing, sitting, and eating.[3]

TYPES OF POWERED MICROMOBILITY VEHICLES[1]

	Powered Bicycle	Powered Standing Scooter	Powered Seated Scooter	Powered Self-Balancing Board	Powered Non-Self-Balancing Board	Powered Skates
Center column	Y	Y	Y	Possible	N	N
Seat	Y	N	Y	N	N	N
Operable pedals	Y	N	N	N	N	N
Floorboard / foot pegs	Possible	Y	Y	Y	Y	Y
Self-balancing[2]	N	N	N	Y	N	Possible

[1] All vehicles typically designed for one person, except for those specifically designed to accommodate additional passenger(s)
[2] Self-balancing refers to dynamic stabilization achieved via a combination of sensors and gyroscopes contained in/on the vehicle

Figure 5-1 Types of Powered Micromobility Vehicles. Self-powered micromobilities can travel faster and farther, and with less effort, than their human-powered equivalents. This expands their potential users and uses. "Self-balancing" refers to dynamic stabilization achieved via a combination of sensors and gyroscopes contained in or on the vehicle. (Source: SAE International from SAE J3194™ Standard—TAXONOMY & CLASSIFICATION OF POWERED MICROMOBILITY VEHICLES. www.sae.org/standards/content/j3194_201911/)

There are many ways to improve and encourage these modes, including building and improving infrastructure such as sidewalks, paths, and bike lanes; reducing motor vehicle traffic speeds through street redesigns; plus supporting compact urban design that locates common destinations within convenient walking and bicycling distances, creating what planners call a "fifteen-minute neighborhood."[4] Communities can adopt *complete streets* policies, which promote roadway designs that accommodate diverse users and uses, particularly active modes, and reduce motor vehicle traffic volumes and speeds.[5] New mapping technologies can evaluate walking and bicycling conditions, and identify where improvements are needed.[6] Improved facility management can reduce conflicts between diverse users on sidewalks and paths.[7]

Current Status

According to the US National Household Travel Survey (NHTS) approximately 12 percent of total trips are made by active modes, but their potential use is much greater.[8] In 2017, approximately 53 percent of all trips were three miles or less, suitable for a fifteen-minute bike or e-scooter ride, and 28 percent of all trips are one mile or less, suitable for a twenty-minute walk.[9] Surveys indicate that many people want to use these modes more often, provided they are convenient and comfortable to use.[10]

There are many reasons for communities to improve and encourage active travel. Affordability, inclusivity, public health, environmental protection, and reduced contagion risk all justify more support for active travel.[11] In response, many communities are improving walking and bicycling facilities and pedestrianizing streets.[12] Some of these programs are specifically designed to help achieve social equity goals.[13] For example, Ohio Safe Routes to Schools programs are targeted toward disadvantaged schools.[14] Affordable housing should be located in walkable and bikeable neighborhoods in order to maximize low-income household's affordability, opportunity, and health.[15]

Active transportation programs currently receive a smaller portion of investments than their mode shares, and far less than their potential mode shares. For example, according to the 2018 *Bicycling and Walking in the United States Benchmarking Report*, less than 2 percent of federal transportation funds, and smaller portions of state transportation funds, are spent on active mode targets.[16] This is far smaller than active modes' share of trips (12 percent) or traffic deaths (19 percent), or what could be justified by comprehensive evaluation of active travel benefits.[17] Many North American communities have ambitious active mode share growth targets. For example, Atlanta, Georgia; Denver, Colorado; Nashville, Tennessee; Pittsburgh, Pennsylvania; St. Petersburg, Florida; and Seattle, Washington, all have targets to approximately double non-auto mode shares; active transportation and micromobility improvements are key to achieving these goals.[18] Many communities are developing pedestrian and bicycle plans,[19] investing in active transport facilities,[20] applying complete streets planning,[21] and implementing Smart Growth policies to create more walkable and bikeable communities.

The User Experience

Under favorable conditions, active and micro modes are enjoyable, but in many situations they are inconvenient and uncomfortable. Many people want to use active modes. According to the 2017 *Outdoor Participation Report*, walking and bicycling are the two most popular outdoor recreation activities: 45 percent of Americans walk, 18 percent run, and 15 percent bike.[22] People who walk or bicycle to work tend to be significantly more satisfied with their commute than those who drive or use public transit.[23] The National Association of Realtors 2017 National Community Preference Survey found that 80 percent of respondents enjoy walking, the most of all travel modes. The survey also found that a majority of households prefer living in a walkable urban neighborhood over automobile-dependent sprawl, and walkable community residents are more satisfied with their quality of life than people living in more automobile-dependent areas.[24]

New analysis tools can be used to evaluate active travel conditions. For example, the Bicycle Level of Traffic Stress (LTS),[25] and walking and bicycling Levels of Quality rating systems can help identify the degree that active transport improvements will provide direct user benefits.[26]

Travel Impacts

Approximately a quarter of total personal trips are less than one mile, and more than half are less than three miles in length, making them suitable for active and micro modes.[27] Improving active travel conditions can significantly increase use of these modes.[28] One major study found that inadequate facilities and heavy vehicle traffic prevent 38 percent of walkers and 45 percent of bikers from using these modes as much as they would like; a lack of sidewalks was a particularly significant barrier to walking in suburbs.[29]

With sufficient facility improvements and incentives, active and micro modes can significantly reduce automobile travel. Active travel improvements can leverage additional vehicle travel reductions, so each additional mile walked or biked causes more than a mile of reduced automobile travel, as summarized in Box 5-1.[30] Installing sidewalks on all streets in a typical North American community would increase per capita walking and cycling by 0.097 average daily miles and reduce automobile travel by 1.142 daily vehicle-miles, about 12 miles of reduced driving for each mile of increased active travel.[31]

Similarly, a Dutch survey found that people who purchase an e-bike significantly increased the distances they travel by bicycle, and reduced their automobile travel about 10 percent..[32] A major academic study, *A Global High Shift Cycling Scenario*, estimated that improving bicycle and e-bike conditions could increase urban bicycling mode shares from the current 6 percent up to 17 percent in 2030 and 22 percent in 2050.[33] Other studies in North America[34] and Europe[35] estimate that, accounting for various climatic and geographic constraints, e-bikes could achieve 10 to 15 percent mode shares and produce up to 12 percent emission reductions in typical urban areas.

BOX 5-1 LEVERAGE EFFECTS OF ACTIVE AND MICROMOBILITIES[i]

Active and micromobility improvements can leverage additional vehicle travel reductions, so each mile of increased walking, scooting, or bicycling reduces more than one vehicle-mile of automobile travel. Following are some mechanisms that can cause this to happen.

- *Shorter trips.* A shorter active trip often substitutes for longer motorized trips, such as when people walk or bike to a local store rather than driving to more distant shops.
- *Reduced chauffeuring.* Improving active travel conditions often allows non-drivers to travel independently, reducing their need to be chauffeured by motorists. Since chauffeuring trips often generate empty backhauls, a mile of walking or bicycling often reduces two vehicle-miles of travel.
- *Increased public transit.* Active travel improvements can support public transit travel, since most transit trips involve active travel links.
- *Vehicle ownership reductions.* Improving alternative modes can allow some households to reduce their vehicle ownership. Since motor vehicles are costly to own but relatively cheap to use, once households purchase an automobile they tend to use it, including many trips that could be made by active modes.
- *Land use patterns.* Walking and bicycling improvements help create more compact, multimodal communities where residents tend to drive less and rely more on other modes.
- *Social norms.* As walking and bicycling increase, so does their social status, further increasing non-auto modes.

Not every active mode improvement has all these effects, but many small changes can help create more multimodal communities. Conventional planning often ignores these leverage effects and so underestimates the potential of active improvements to achieve goals such as congestion reduction, traffic safety, and environmental protection.

[i] Litman (2019). *Evaluating Active Transport Benefits and Costs.* Victoria Transport Policy Institute, www.vtpi.org/nmt-tdm.pdf.

Benefits and Costs

Active modes and micro modes tend to have relatively low speeds, although, as discussed in chapter 3, because of their affordability, their *effective speeds* (travel distance divided by time spent traveling plus earning money to pay for travel) are often comparable to motorized modes, and under favorable conditions their travel time unit costs (dollars per hour) are lower than motorized travel due to their enjoyment and health benefits.[36] As a result, travelers often choose to use active or micro modes, even if a trip takes somewhat longer or they must choose closer destinations.

Active and micro mode improvements can help achieve social equity objectives. The article "'Paying to Stay Safe': Why Women Don't Walk as Much as Men" found that fear of harassment and assault deter women from walking, reducing their independence, health, and affordability. The discrepancy between men's and women's walking activity declined in more compact and walkable communities, indicating that a comprehensive set of active mode improvements help reduce mobility inequity.[37] One major study using income and travel data for more than 3.66 million Americans found that children born in lower-income families are much more likely to become economically successful adults if they grow up in walkable urban neighborhoods rather than automobile dependent areas.[38] It also found that economically disadvantaged workers have much smaller employment and income disparities in walkable cities, indicating that improving active travel helps increase economic opportunity.

Active and micro modes tend to have low user and infrastructure costs, providing savings and benefits to travelers and communities. A scooter or bicycle costs $100 to $500, and an e-scooter or e-bike costs $400 to $2,000. Micromobilities can travel faster than walking and farther than human-powered bicycles, with lower costs than automobiles. Active transportation infrastructure costs are tiny compared with total expenditures to build and maintain roadways and parking facilities for motor vehicles.[39] Federal and state transportation agencies typically spend less than 2 percent of their budget on bicycle and pedestrian facilities, far smaller than their mode shares, suggesting that current planning underinvests in active modes.[40] The incremental costs of active transport infrastructure improvements are usually repaid by health benefits from increased physical fitness and reduced pollution.[41]

By reducing motor vehicle traffic, active and micro modes can also reduce traffic and parking congestions. One study of twenty pedestrian and bicycle improvement projects found that ten clearly reduced vehicle traffic congestion, eight had no measurable effect, and two caused slight congestion increases.[42] By improving connections between parking spaces and destinations, walkability improvements tend to increase convenience for motorists and reduce parking problems. Because these modes are affordable and easy to use, they help achieve equity goals, particularly if targeted at disadvantaged groups—for example, by improving sidewalks and bicycle facilities in lower-income neighborhoods.[43] Active mode users can be vulnerable to crash injuries but impose minimal risk on other travelers, so total crash rates tend to decline as their mode shares increase, an effect called "safety in numbers."[44] These modes can experience conflicts with other sidewalk, path, and road users, and so may require new regulations and education programs.

Active modes increase public fitness and health.[45] For example, one major study of 263,450 UK commuters found that, controlling for other demographic factors, those who walk or bicycle have lower cardiovascular disease risk, and those who bicycle have lower cancer risk and increased longevity.[46] There is also evidence that active transport provides psychological benefits. Using British Household Panel Survey data and accounting for potential confounding variables relating to work, residence, and health, researchers found that overall psychological well-being was significantly higher for active mode commuters compared to car travel and public transit users.[47] Put simply, frequent walking and bicycling tends to make people healthy and happy.

Because they are unenclosed, active modes have minimal contagion risk. During the COVID-19 pandemic, many cities expanded their walking and bicycling facilities in order to reduce crowding and accommodate more active travel.[48] By reducing total vehicle travel, encouraging compact development, and minimizing pavement area, they help achieve strategic planning goals.

Roles

Active and micro mode improvements can provide efficient, affordable, and healthy mobility and improve access to public transit and parking facilities. Some improvements, such as streetscaping and traffic calming, also enhance neighborhood livability. Active mode improvements are particularly beneficial in lower-income and minority neighborhoods. They can be targeted to improve children's access to schools, parks, and recreational facilities. The US Department of Transportation, and many states and cities, have Safe Routes to Schools programs that improve and encourage active travel by students, parents, and staff.[49] Although dense urban areas tend to have the highest rates of active and micro modes, there is latent demand for these modes in suburban and rural areas. Active and micro modes can support and be supported by other New Mobilities including vehicle sharing, public transit improvements, ridehailing, Mobility as a Service, mobility prioritization, and logistics management, particularly cargo-bike delivery services.

Vehicle Sharing

Vehicle sharing refers to bicycle, e-scooter, e-bike, and car rental services intended to substitute for private ownership.[50] These services are designed and located for maximum convenience and priced for shorter trips. Some allow one-way travel (picking up a vehicle in one location and leaving it elsewhere) for additional convenience.

Local governments can encourage carsharing by allowing bike and scooter parking in public areas, giving carsharing preferred access to public parking facilities, and reducing parking minimums in exchange for vehicle sharing services in buildings.[51] Public transit agencies can integrate scooter-, bike-, and carsharing into train stations and other mobility hubs.[52]

Current Status

Commercial carsharing started in North America with Zipcar in 2000 and has since matured and expanded into new markets. Bikeshare services developed in most large cities between 2010 and 2015, but many subsequently declined due to high costs and inadequate demand, or have evolved into scooter-sharing.[53] They tend to be most successful in dense urban areas and if supported by public policies, including favorable parking policies or financial subsidies.[54]

The User Experience

Carsharing is generally more convenient than conventional vehicle rentals, due to more locations and quicker pick-up and drop-off transactions, but is less convenient than having a personal vehicle. Under favorable conditions, with well-maintained vehicles and appropriate facilities, scooter- and bikesharing can be convenient, comfortable, and fun.

Travel Impacts

Vehicle sharing can significantly reduce automobile ownership and travel, particularly in multimodal areas with diverse travel options.[55] Shifting from car ownership to carsharing increases the variable-cost of driving from about ten cents to about fifty cents per mile, which gives travelers a strong incen-tive to minimize their vehicle travel. Motorists who shift from owning a car to car-sharing typically reduce their annual mileage by 40 to 60 percent.[56] Bikesharing can substitute for automobile travel for some trips. One major study found that 5.5 percent of bikeshare users reduced their vehicle ownership, 50 percent reduced their vehicle travel, and 58 percent increased their bicycle travel.[57]

Benefits and Costs

Carsharing is generally cost effective for people who drive less than about five thousand annual miles. By providing an affordable mobility option, vehicle sharing can help achieve social equity goals, particularly if services are oriented toward disadvantaged groups. To make them more inclusive, experts recommend that car- and bikeshare services be located, priced, and marketed to lower-income and minority groups and be integrated with facility improvements and public transit services.[58]

By reducing automobile ownership and travel, vehicle sharing helps reduce traffic congestion, road and parking facility costs, crashes, and pollution emissions.[59] Because most carsharing vehicles only have a few passengers each week and are often parked for hours between users, their contagion risk is moderate. Because shared scooters and bikes are unenclosed, their contagion risk is low. During the COVID-19 pandemic, most vehicle-sharing services increased cleaning practices to further reduce risks. By reducing total vehicle travel and sprawl they help achieve strategic planning goals.

Roles

Vehicle sharing can provide a convenient and affordable alternative to vehicle ownership. Such programs are particularly appropriate in denser, multimodal communities.[60] If oriented toward lower-income communities they can help achieve social equity goals, including affordability, more independent mobility, and (for bikesharing) improved fitness and health. Bike- and scooter-sharing can provide an affordable local mobility option and improve public transit access.[61] To be most effective, vehicle sharing must be part of overall efforts to reduce private automobile ownership and use. For example, carsharing becomes more successful and beneficial if parking is unbundled, so car-free households are no longer forced to pay for costly parking spaces they don't need. Scooter- and bikesharing are more successful and beneficial if implemented with active transport facility improvements and complete streets policies.

Ridehailing and Microtransit

Ridehailing companies (also called *ridesourcing* and *transportation network companies*, or *TNCs*), such as Uber and Lyft, use smartphone apps to provide personal mobility services. *Microtransit* uses vans and small buses to provide mobility services to multiple passengers.[62]

Current Status

Ridehailing began in 2009 with the establishment of UberCab. The industry is still developing and expanding to include more companies, services (goods deliveries, special vehicles, and microtransit), and areas.[63] Ridehailing services compete with conventional taxis but are generally less regulated and more technologically sophisticated, which allows them to be more efficient and affordable, with prices that are typically 20 to 40 percent lower than taxis.[64] Many ridehailing companies are currently unprofitable, and some jurisdictions are reforming taxi and ridehailing regulations, so their service and price advantages may change as the industry matures.[65]

The User Experience

Ridehailing and microtransit tend to be more convenient and comfortable than conventional public transit services for many types of trips. Their apps tend to be more convenient than conventional taxi services, but this discrepancy is declining as taxi companies adopt new technologies. Flexible-route microtransit can reduce the distances that passengers must walk to stops, resulting in more convenience than conventional, fixed-route transit services.

Travel Impacts

Ridehailing can have various travel impacts.[66] It allows some households to reduce their vehicle ownership, which leverages vehicle travel reductions, but often increases vehicle travel by replacing walking, bicycling, and public transit trips, and by generating empty backhauls (vehicle travel without passengers). A major North American study found that 60 percent of ridehail passengers would otherwise have used a personal vehicle or taxi, and about 40 percent would have walked, biked, or taken public transit.[67] This suggests that, with current policies, ridehailing tends to increase vehicle travel overall.

Microtransit can provide efficient, shared mobility that can reduce vehicle travel. However, commercial microtransit services only operate on high-demand corridors, which can reduce the profitability and quality of conventional public transit, which may increase total vehicle travel over the long run.[68]

Benefits and Costs

Ridehailing and microtransit are generally faster and more convenient than conventional public transit services but slower than using a personal vehicle. They tend to be cheaper than taxi travel but more expensive than public transit.[69] Where they increase total vehicle travel they tend to increase traffic congestion, infrastructure costs, crashes, and pollution emissions.[70] They tend to have mixed social equity impacts: they provide an affordable mobility option for some low-income travelers, but by reducing public transit ridership they can reduce transit system efficiency and lead to reduced transit service over the long term. Many ridehailing drivers appreciate its flexibility (they can choose their work hours) but dislike its low wages and lack of benefits.[71] If ridehailing trips replace walking, bicycling, and public transit travel, they are likely to reduce public fitness and health. Because many people occupy each vehicle every day, ridehailing and microtransit are likely to have high contagion risk. By increasing total vehicle travel and sprawl, they tend to contradict strategic planning goals unless implemented with vehicle travel reduction and anti-sprawl policies.

Most public transit agencies provide special demand response microtransit services for people with mobility impairments, and a few have tested demand response services for general users, but the response times and costs of these services tend to be high. For example, SW Prime, which provides curb-to-curb on-demand services during weekdays in suburban Minneapolis, has a 1.85-hour average wait time, averages just 3.4 passengers per hour, and requires an $8.00 average subsidy per passenger.[72]

Roles

Ridehailing and microtransit can provide convenient and relatively affordable mobility for many trips. To prevent them from increasing total vehicle travel and reducing public transit services, ridehailing and microtransit should be implemented with policies that encourage shared travel and discourage vehicle traffic growth such as high-occupancy vehicle (HOV) lanes, decongestion pricing (tolls on congested roads),[73] efficient curb management,[74] and public transit service improvements.

Electric Vehicles

Electric vehicles include battery-electric e-scooters, e-bikes, mobility scooters, motorcycles, automobiles, buses, and trucks.

Current Status

Battery-electric vehicles first developed in the late 1800s but were uncommon during most of the twentieth century. In the 1990s, some vehicle manufacturers developed improved models, and by 2020 most major producers sold electric cars with performance (reliability, speed, carrying capacity, and range) comparable to fossil fuel vehicles. High-performance models are currently expensive but becoming more affordable.[75] Electric scooters, bicycles, motorcycles, buses, and trucks are also improving in performance and affordability. Currently, in North America fewer than 2 percent of new vehicles are electric, but their market share is growing.[76] Many jurisdictions offer electric vehicle purchase incentives.[77] Many public transit agencies are starting to purchase electric buses, and some governments and businesses are purchasing electric vehicles for their fleets.

The User Experience

Battery-powered electric vehicles are quieter and less polluting than fossil fuel vehicles, and so tend to be more comfortable. However, most have less range than fossil fuel vehicles, and the supply of public charging stations is currently limited. E-scooters, e-bikes, and mobility scooters require less effort, and so can travel faster and farther than their human-powered equivalents.

Travel Impacts

Electric vehicle operating costs are about half of equivalent fossil fuel vehicles,[78] which is likely to increase their annual mileage by 10 to 30 percent.[79]

Benefits and Costs

An electric vehicle currently costs several thousand dollars more to purchase than a comparable fossil fuel vehicle but is cheaper to operate.[80] A typical electric car uses three to twelve cents worth of electricity per mile, about half the fuel costs of an equivalent gasoline car.[81] Their batteries must be replaced about every one hundred thousand miles, which currently costs $3,000 to $15,000 or three to ten cents per vehicle-mile. E-scooters and e-bikes are more expensive than their human-powered equivalents but cheaper than automobiles.

Electric vehicles reduce noise and air pollution[82] and the external costs of producing and distributing fossil fuels.[83] Their batteries add significant weight (often more than one thousand pounds), which increases tire noise and particulate pollution.[84] In many jurisdictions, electric vehicles receive purchase subsidies and subsidized recharging stations, and because they do not pay special vehicle fuel taxes, their roadway costs are subsidized. Because of their low operating costs they tend to increase total vehicle travel, which increases traffic congestion, infrastructure, and crash costs. Their subsidies tend to be regressive (lower-income people's taxes tend to subsidize wealthy motorists), which contradicts equity goals, although this should decline as electric vehicles become more affordable. Electric-assist bicycles increase public fitness and health compared with automobile travel but less than non-assisted bicycles. Because e-scooters, e-bikes, and electric motorcycles are unenclosed they have lower contagion risk than automobile and public transit travel. Electric cars tend to contradict strategic planning goals by increasing total vehicle travel and sprawl, while e-bikes and e-scooters tend to support these goals by favoring shorter trips and compact development.

Roles

Electric vehicles are particularly beneficial when used for high-annual-mileage applications such as taxis, buses, service vehicles, and freight trucks operating in dense urban areas where noise and air pollution problems are severe.[85] E-scooters and e-bikes can serve many local trips, and electric motorcycles can significantly reduce noise and air pollution in cities where two-wheelers are common.

Autonomous Vehicles

Autonomous (also called *self-driving* or *robotic*) vehicles are automobiles, buses, freight trucks, and local delivery vehicles that can operate without a human driver.[86] The Society of Automotive Engineers (SAE) defines various levels of autonomy, as summarized in Table 5-1. Levels 2–4 vehicles can operate autonomously in certain conditions but require a qualified driver ready to take control when needed. Level 5 (full automation) vehicles can operate autonomously under all normal conditions, and so can carry people who cannot drive and can travel unoccupied to reposition or carry goods. Many benefits, such as independent mobility for nondrivers and more affordable bus, freight, and taxi services, require Level 5 capability.[87]

Table 5-1 Autonomous Vehicle Levels[i]. The Society of Automotive Engineers defines five levels of vehicle automation. Levels 2–4 reduce stress but still require a qualified driver available at the wheel. Many benefits require Level 5 (full automation).

Level	*1* *Driver* *Assistance*	*2* *Partial* *Automation*	*3–4* *Conditional* *Automation*	*5* *Full* *Automation*
	Single automated system, such as cruise control	Some automated control under some conditions	Can self-drive in some conditions, such as limited-access highways	Can self-drive under all normal conditions
Current status	Common (e.g., cruise control)	Limited availability (e.g., autopilot)	Design and testing	Design and testing
Costs	Low	Moderate	High equipment costs	High equipment and operating costs
Driver Required?	Yes	Yes	Yes	No

[i] SAE (2018). "Taxonomy and Definitions for Terms Related to Driving Automation Systems for On-Road Motor Vehicles." Society of Automotive Engineers, www.sae.org/standards/content/j3016 _201806.

Table 5-2 Ownership and Operating Models Compared. Autonomous vehicles can be private or shared. Each model has advantages and disadvantages.

	Private Autonomous Vehicles	Shared Autonomous Vehicles	Shared Autonomous Rides
	Households own or lease self-driving vehicles	*Self-driving taxis serve individuals*	*Microtransit serves multiple passengers*
Advantages	• High convenience • Always available • Users can leave gear in vehicles • Pride of ownership	• Users can choose vehicles that best meet their needs • Door-to-door service	• Lowest total costs • Minimizes congestion risk and pollution emissions
Disadvantages	• High costs • Users cannot choose different vehicles for different uses • Likely to increase vehicle travel and associated costs including congestion, roadway costs, crashes, and pollution emissions	• Users must wait for vehicles • Limited services (no driver to help passengers carry luggage or ensure safety)	• Least speed, convenience, and comfort, particularly in sprawled areas
Appropriate Users	• Affluent suburban and rural residents	• Lower-annual-mileage users	• Lower-income urban residents

There are various possible ownership and operating models: households could own or lease a private autonomous vehicle, they could use autonomous taxis to transport individuals or groups, or they could travel with other passengers in autonomous microtransit or buses. Each has advantages and disadvantages, as summarized in Table 5-2.

Current Status

Autonomous vehicles are currently under development. Many vehicles now have Level 2 abilities, such as cruise control and automatic parking, but significant progress is needed before vehicles can operate reliably in mixed traffic, in heavy rain and snow, and on unpaved roads, and years of testing will be required before they are approved for general use.[88]

This suggests that Level 5 autonomous vehicles, able to operate without a driver, may be commercially available in some jurisdictions by the late 2020s, but the first generations will probably be expensive and have limited abilities—for example, unable to operate in inclement weather or reach destinations on unpaved roads or in unmapped areas.[89] This will limit sales, since many consumers may be reluctant to pay significantly higher prices for a vehicle with limited capabilities. Some benefits, such as independent mobility for affluent non-drivers, may begin in the 2030s or 2040s, but most impacts, including reduced traffic and parking congestion, independent mobility for low-income people (and therefore reduced public transit demand), increased safety, energy conservation, and pollution reductions, will only be significant when autonomous vehicles become affordable and common, probably in the 2040s to 2050s, and some benefits may require prohibiting human-driven vehicles on certain roadways, which could take even longer.

The User Experience

Autonomous vehicles allow occupants to rest or work while traveling. However, they can introduce new stresses and discomforts. Travelers may experience "access anxiety" if vehicles are sometimes unable to reach desired destinations. Self-driving taxis and microtransit will lack operators, and so cannot provide passenger assistance and security, such as carrying baggage, local knowledge, or ensuring that passengers safely reach their destinations. To minimize vandalism and misbehavior they will be designed with hardened surfaces, such as chrome and plastic, and equipped with security cameras. Despite these precautions, autonomous taxis will require frequent cleaning and repairs, and passengers may often encounter previous occupants' garbage, stains, and odors.[90] As a result, some travelers may choose to pay a premium for taxis and buses with human operators.

Travel Impacts

Autonomous vehicles can increase vehicle travel in several ways.[91] They facilitate vehicle travel by people who cannot drive. By increasing passenger comfort and productivity, they can make long-distance trips more endurable, increasing vehicle travel and sprawl. They can add empty vehicle-miles—for example, if motorists direct their cars home or to circle the block to avoid paying parking fees. Because they will cost more to own but less to drive than current automobiles, they increase vehicle owners' incentive to maximize their mileage in order to get their money's worth from their large fixed investments.

People may reduce their vehicle travel if they shift from owning personal vehicles to relying on autonomous taxi and microtransit service. However, many people have good reasons to own rather than share vehicles, whether or not they are autonomous. A personal vehicle is convenient; it is always available and can be loaded with personal items such as child seats, tools, and special racks to carry sports equipment or wheelchairs. Many workers leave tools and supplies in their vehicles. In addition, many motorists take pride in their cars. Although taxi dispatching generally requires just a few minutes in dense urban areas, it can take much longer in sprawled suburban and rural areas. As a result, urban residents will be more likely to rely on autonomous taxis and reduce their mileage, while suburban and rural residents will be more likely to own autonomous vehicles and increase their mileage. Of course, these impacts are difficult to predict and will depend on other factors, including policies that affect the relative costs of private and shared vehicle travel.

Studies of these factors suggest that, with current policies, autonomous vehicles are likely to increase affected vehicle travel by 10 to 30 percent, and possibly more, but with TDM incentives that encourage shared mobility and compact development, such as high-occupancy vehicle lanes and decongestion road tolls, they can reduce total vehicle travel.[92]

Benefits and Costs

Under most conditions, autonomous vehicles are likely to have travel speeds comparable to human-operated automobiles. They may be slower than human-operated vehicles if they are programmed to maximize passenger comfort or strictly follow traffic rules, or if they frequently stop and wait for human intervention when faced with unexpected conditions. They can be faster than human-operated vehicles if given dedicated lanes that allow platooning (numerous vehicles driving close together at higher speeds). Because passengers can relax or be productive, their travel time unit costs will be reduced. For example, autonomous vehicle users may take longer duration trips knowing that they can rest or work while traveling. Autonomous taxi and microtransit trips generally take longer than personal vehicle travel, particularly in suburban and rural areas where response times may be high, but often take less time than conventional public transit services. They can provide independent mobility for non-drivers, which helps achieve social equity goals.

Autonomous vehicles require additional equipment and services, such as sophisticated control systems and specialized mapping. Since failures can be deadly, autonomous vehicles need robust components maintained by specialists, which will increase maintenance and repair costs. If they follow the pattern of previous vehicle technologies, autonomous driving capability will initially be available in higher-priced models and will eventually be incorporated into most new vehicles. This suggests that autonomous driving capabilities will add a few thousand dollars in annualized expenses during the first few decades of their commercial availability, until competition and depreciation make these technologies available in lower-priced and used vehicles.

Some optimists predict that autonomous taxi services will cost just twenty cents per vehicle-mile and autonomous microtransit services just ten cents per passenger-mile,[93] making them cheap enough to be funded by advertising.[94] However, these estimates are unrealistically low because they ignore many costs required to operate such services, including frequent cleaning, vandalism repairs, safety and security monitoring, road user fees, management, profits, and deadhead (empty vehicle travel) miles. For every one hundred revenue-miles, taxis typically require sixty to one hundred additional vehicle-miles to pick up and drop off passengers, and ridehailing companies currently charge about 25 percent for administration and profit.[95] This suggests that even if autonomous electric vehicles only cost twenty cents per vehicle-mile to operate, autonomous taxis will need to charge fares of fifty to eighty cents per vehicle-mile, and microtransit twenty-five to forty cents per passenger-mile, in order to pay all overhead and deadhead travel costs, and earn a profit, which is cheaper than human-operated taxis and ridehailing but more expensive than driving a personal vehicle or riding conventional public transit.[96] Figure 5-2 compares these costs.

Autonomous technologies can make taxi, microtransit, and bus services more affordable, which can help achieve social equity goals including independent mobility for non-drivers and cost savings for lower-income travelers. However, if they increase total vehicle travel, autonomous vehicles are likely to increase total traffic congestion, infrastructure costs (particularly if they require roadway transponders or special lanes), and

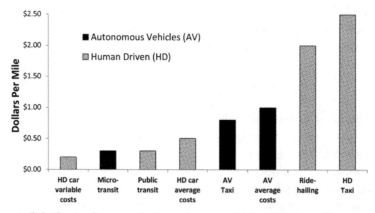

Figure 5-2 Costs Compared. Autonomous vehicles (AVs) are likely to cost more than human-driven (HD) vehicles, but less than human-driven taxis and ridehailing services. Variable costs affect short-term travel decisions. Average costs include all vehicle expenses.

pollution emissions. Those vehicles can experience less congestion if given dedicated lanes that allow platooning, but that is only justified where autonomous vehicles are common, and if autonomous lanes displace general traffic lanes they may increase congestion for human-operated vehicles. They can reduce parking costs if travelers shift from personal vehicles to autonomous taxis or microtransit, or if autonomous vehicle owners program their cars to return home or drive in circles on public roads, although that would increase congestion, crash, and pollution costs.

Optimists claim that because human error contributes to 90 percent of crashes, autonomous operation will prevent most crashes, but this overlooks additional risks these technologies can introduce, including hardware and software failures, malicious hacking, platooning dangers that may cause large multi-vehicle pileups, special risks to pedestrians and bicyclists, and additional crashes caused by increased vehicle travel.[97] Because they are enclosed and shared vehicles, autonomous taxi and microtransit travel is likely to have moderate to high contagion risk. By increasing total vehicle travel and sprawl they contradict strategic planning goals.

Roles

Autonomous operation is particularly appropriate for commercial and shared vehicles, including microtransit, buses, and taxis. Private autonomous vehicles are appropriate for affluent high-annual-mileage motorists and non-drivers. Autonomous taxis and microtransit can offer affordable and efficient mobility, particularly in denser urban areas.

Public Transit Innovations

Public transit innovations include various technologies that improve transit travel convenience, comfort, and efficiency. These include transit navigation and payment apps, transit priority control systems, nicer vehicles and stations, faster service, and amenities such as on-board Wi-Fi, plus integrated programs such as *bus rapid transit* (BRT), *high-speed rail* (HSR), and *personal rapid transit* (PRT) systems. It can also include TDM incentives that encourage transit ridership, and transit-oriented development (TOD) policies that increase the portion of houses and businesses located close to frequent transit services.

Current Status

Various transit innovations are developing and maturing. Most transit systems have navigation apps; a few have electronic payment systems.[98] Some are deploying advanced control systems that give transit priority at intersections. Many transit agencies are starting to operate electric buses and offer amenities such as on-board Wi-Fi services. BRT planning practices are now well established,[99] and many cities are expanding and improving BRT systems.[100] Several countries have extensive HSR networks.[101] A few PRT systems exist, but they are experiencing little growth.[102] Many jurisdictions are implementing transit-oriented development policies.

The User Experience

Transit innovations and TOD policies can significantly improve travelers' convenience and comfort. They reduce delay and crowding, improve user information and payment options, increase passenger comfort, provide enjoyable amenities, and improve the overall accessibility of transit.

Travel Impacts

By improving transit travel convenience and comfort, transit innovations can increase ridership and reduce automobile travel. An integrated package of transit service improvements, supportive TDM policies, and TOD policies can reduce affected residents and commuters' automobile travel by 40 to 60 percent.[103]

Transit ridership tends to increase significantly in cities that develop major new rail or bus rapid transit systems.[104] Some cities, such as Seattle, Washington,[105] and Houston, Texas,[106] have increased transit ridership with incremental improvements that include bus lanes, more efficient and frequent service, and more convenient user information.

Benefits and Costs

Public transit improvements can provide numerous benefits, including affordable mobility, efficient travel on busy urban corridors, and environmental benefits, plus additional long-term benefits if they are a catalyst for more compact and multimodal urban development.[107] Public transit is generally slower than automobile travel, but many transit improvements increase travel speed, convenience, and comfort. Because passengers can relax and work, many travelers will choose a comfortable bus or train over a faster automobile trip. Transit-oriented development can increase overall accessibility, reducing residents' overall travel time costs.

Public transit improvements can provide user savings and affordability benefits; a monthly transit pass typically costs a fraction of the total costs of owning and operating an automobile. By reducing vehicle traffic on major urban corridors, transit improvements can significantly reduce traffic congestion, infrastructure costs, crashes, and pollution emissions. By improving user convenience and comfort, and providing independent mobility for non-drivers and an affordable mobility option, they help achieve social equity goals. Because most transit trips include walking and bicycling links, and TOD improves walking and bicycling conditions, these improvements tend to increase public fitness and health. Because multiple passengers travel in enclosed vehicles, transit travel tends to have contagion risk, although current research indicates that this is moderate and can be reduced with appropriate policies.[108] Public transit and transit-oriented development strongly support strategic planning goals, including vehicle travel reductions and more compact development. Some transit improvements are costly and require ongoing subsidies. Table 5-3 summarizes various benefits and costs of public transit improvements and transit-oriented development.

Table 5-3 Public Transit Benefits and Costs[i].

	Improved Transit Service	Increased Transit Travel	Reduced Automobile Travel	Transit-Oriented Development
Metrics	*Service Quality (speed, reliability, comfort, safety, etc.)*	*Transit Ridership Passenger-miles (or mode share)*	*Mode Shifts or Automobile Travel Reductions*	*Portion of Development with TOD Design Features*
Potential Benefits	• Improved convenience and comfort for existing users • Equity benefits (since existing users tend to be disadvantaged) • Option value (the value of having an option for possible future use) • Improved operating efficiency (if service speed increases) • Improved security (reduced crime risk)	• Mobility benefits to new users • Increased fare revenue • Increased public fitness and health (by stimulating more walking or cycling trips) • Increased security as more people ride transit and wait at stops and stations	• Reduced traffic congestion • Road and parking facility cost savings • Consumer savings • Reduced chauffeuring burdens • Increased traffic safety • Energy conservation • Air and noise pollution reductions	• Additional vehicle travel reductions ("leverage effects") • Improved accessibility, particularly for non-drivers • Community cohesion and reduced crime risk • More efficient development (reduced infrastructure costs) • Farmland and habitat preservation
Potential Costs	• Higher capital and operating costs and therefore subsidies • Land and road space • Traffic congestion and accident risk imposed by transit vehicles	• Transit vehicle crowding	• Reduced automobile business activity	• Problems associated with more compact development, such as more intense congestion and more concentrated noise and air pollution

[i] Todd Litman (2020). *Evaluating Public Transit Benefits and Costs.* Victoria Transport Policy Institute, www.vtpi.org/tranben.pdf.

Roles

Public transit improvements can play many roles in an efficient and equitable transportation system, including affordable basic mobility for non-drivers, resource-efficient urban mobility, and serving as a catalyst for compact and multimodal neighborhoods. Transit improvements support and are supported by TDM incentives and Smart Growth development policies.

Mobility as a Service (MaaS)

Mobility as a Service (MaaS, also called *Mobility on Demand*) uses mobile apps to provide integrated trip planning and payment for multiple modes, including walking, bicycling, vehicle sharing, taxi, ridehailing, and public transit, plus vehicle parking and toll payment.[109] It allows travelers to easily identify and compare travel options, make reservations, use services, obtain support, and make payments—for example, coordinating a bike-bus-ridehailing trip. Some systems indicate the carbon footprint and caloric output of travel options or link to games and rewards to encourage users to choose resource-efficient modes. It can be integrated with physical infrastructure, such as *mobility hubs*, which are centers that seamlessly connect various sustainable transportation modes, typically including high-quality public transit, plus vehicle rental services and passenger amenities.[110]

Current Status

MaaS is now commercially available and expanding in many markets.[111] The concept was developed in 2014 by MaaS Global, which released the award-winning Whim app in 2016, and subsequently expanded into markets around the world.[112] Some older urban mobility apps, such as City Mapper, GoogleMaps, and Moovel provide information on multiple travel modes, but currently lack MaaS features such as integrated payment.[113]

The User Experience

MaaS can significantly improve the convenience, comfort, and security of non-auto travel by providing integrated navigation and payment systems for multiple mobility options. Users generally need a smart-phone and a credit card account.

Travel Impacts

By improving the convenience of non-auto modes, MaaS can significantly reduce automobile ownership and use. According to some predictions, when integrated mobility services are fully developed, vehicle ownership will decline by half.[114] MaaS supports and is supported by improvements to resource-efficient modes including active and public transportation, vehicle sharing, and ridehailing.

Benefits and Costs

MaaS increases the convenience of multimodal travel. This can provide direct savings and benefits to users and, by improving lower-priced travel options, tends to increase affordability. By helping to reduce automobile ownership and use, it can reduce traffic and parking congestion, infrastructure costs, crashes, and pollution emissions. By improving mobility options for disadvantaged groups, it tends to support social equity goals. If it encourages more walking and bicycling, it helps increase public fitness and health. By reducing total vehicle travel and encouraging compact development, it tends to achieve strategic planning goals. However, if it significantly expands microtransit, it could reduce higher-capacity public transit.[115] Its costs include data and payment standardization, interorganizational coordination, and software development. If it collects users' travel data, it may raise privacy concerns.

Roles

MaaS is a cost-effective way to support efficient mobility. It should be implemented in conjunction with other New Mobilities including active travel, vehicle sharing, public transit innovations, and ridehailing improvements.[116] It requires public support. For example, Finland requires all public and private mobility service providers to integrate their data and payment systems in a standardized format in order to create an open and competitive market for mobility services.[117]

Telework

Telework refers to telecommunications that substitute for physical travel, including *telecommuting* (working from home), *e-business* (online sales, banking, and other commercial services), *e-medicine* or *telehealth* (internet-based medical services), and *e-government* (online public services).[118]

Current Status

Hardware, software, internet, and delivery service improvements make telework appropriate for an increasing range of users and uses. However, there is significant potential for further development.[119] The COVID-19 pandemic significantly increased all types of teleworking. It caused the portion of employees who work at home, at least occasionally, to increase from about a quarter to nearly half.[120] It also significantly increased use of e-learning, e-commerce, e-government, and e-medicine. Some of these changes are likely to continue into the future.

The User Experience

Under optimal conditions, telework can be convenient and enjoyable, but it is sometimes difficult and frustrating due to hardware and software problems, inadequate human support, and poor integration. It also reduces human interaction and therefore the opportunities for learning and socializing that occur when people interact face to face.

Travel Impacts

An estimated half of US workers are in occupations in which teleworking is feasible at least part-time.[121] Telework can significantly reduce participating employees' commute travel.[122] For example, a twice-a-week teleworker generates 40 percent fewer commute trips. However, these reductions are often offset by various rebound effects: teleworkers may make additional errand trips that would have been made during a commute; employees may use telework to move further from their worksites, which increases travel distances and sprawl; telecommuters may use additional energy for heating, cooling, and electronic equipment; and online shopping and telework document delivery can generate additional vehicle trips.[123] Research suggests that telework tends to increase total mobility and energy use unless implemented with vehicle travel reduction and anti-sprawl policies.[124]

Benefits and Costs

Telework reduces travel time costs but may require additional time for online communications and transactions. Under favorable conditions it can save money and improve employee and customer satisfaction, productivity, and economic opportunities, but if used inappropriately it can increase costs and harm workers, particularly for disadvantaged groups who lack necessary equipment, space, and skills. For example, it can be stressful to study or work in a crowded house that lacks a suitable workspace, some people feel lonely or isolated working alone, and many people find it difficult to operate the technologies required for effective telework.

By reducing commuting trips, telework can reduce traffic congestion but often increases other types of vehicle travel.[125] Its equity impacts depend on how it is implemented: if optional it can benefit disadvantaged people, but it may be harmful if imposed on inappropriate workers or clients, such as people who lack high-speed internet, live in crowded houses, or lack technical skills. It can significantly reduce exposure to infectious diseases and so is particularly appropriate during pandemics.

Roles

Telework can provide efficient services and employment opportunities but is unsuitable for many types of work and workers. It can be appropriate for people with disabilities or living in isolated areas, provided they receive adequate equipment and support. It minimizes contagion risks and so is particularly helpful for people who are immunocompromised or during epidemics. Because it can provide many benefits, public policies should support telework where appropriate, but since it can increase total travel, it should be implemented in conjunction with TDM and compact development policies. Employers, businesses, and governments should develop telework policies and programs and provide appropriate support. Telework should generally be optional rather than required.

Tunnel Roads and Pneumatic Tube Transport

The Boring Company proposes to solve urban traffic congestion by creating a network of tunnel roads that allow high-speed vehicle travel beneath cities.[126] It claims that new construction technologies will allow these tunnels to meet all engineering and environmental requirements and earn a profit from user fees.

Hyperloop Transportation Technologies (TT) proposes building a network of pneumatic tubes that transport passengers between cities in pressurized capsules traveling at approximately the speed of sound.[127]

Current Status

These modes are currently in conceptual and development stages. Although tunnel roads and pneumatic tube systems can be built with existing technologies, significant advancements are needed to achieve the performance and cost efficiency required for their commercial success.[128] Even if new technologies can significantly reduce construction costs, these modes are likely to have high operating costs, including tunnel and station maintenance, air circulation, safety and security, and insurance. The Boring Company has built prototype tunnels[129] and Hyperloop TT has built prototype pneumatic tubes[130] but neither has yet to demonstrate large-scale commercial potential. A NASA expert review, *Hyperloop Commercial Feasibility Analysis: High Level Overview*, concluded that Hyperloop costs are likely to be much higher, and its performance and profitability much lower, than proponents claim.[131] Conventional toll roads are seldom profitable because the prices needed to recover costs greatly reduce demand; tunnel roads and pneumatic tube transport are likely to face similar constraints.[132] As a result, these modes are likely to be profitable on only a few high-volume corridors.

The User Experience

These modes will probably be inconvenient and uncomfortable for most trips. Passengers will travel in confined spaces, without natural light or fresh air, and some passengers may experience claustrophobia or nausea. Their networks will have limited access points and so will serve a limited number of destinations and trip types.

Travel Impacts

The travel impacts of these modes will depend on their ultimate comfort, price, and scale of their networks. If tunnel roads become as fast, affordable, and extensive as proponents predict, providing high-speed, inexpensive automobile travel beneath numerous cities, they are likely to increase total vehicle travel and sprawl.[133] If they attract travelers who would otherwise drive or fly, pneumatic tube transport may reduce vehicle travel on some corridors.

Benefits and Costs

Tunnel and tube transportation can increase travel speed for some trips, although door-to-door time savings may be modest for destinations that are not near their access points and stations. These modes are costly to build and operate and so will require substantial tolls and fares to recover costs, or they will require significant public subsidies. Although Elon Musk once predicted twenty-dollar Hyperloop fares between Los Angeles and San Francisco, his analysis overlooked many costs and assumed 100 percent load factors (every seat is always filled).[134] Actual fares are likely to be many times higher. As a result, they are unlikely to provide significant consumer savings compared with automobile, bus, or air travel, and any subsidies are likely to be regressive, benefiting affluent travelers at the expense of lower-income taxpayers. Construction of tunnels and pneumatic tubes is likely to impose significant external costs (infrastructure and habitat disruption, noise, dust, etc.). If they offer fast and affordable driving conditions, tunnel roads are likely to induce additional vehicle travel that will increase downstream congestion, crash risk, and pollution emissions. In theory, pneumatic tube transport can be energy efficient, but its actual performance has yet to be tested. If this mode substitutes for air travel it could significantly reduce noise and air pollution.[135] These modes will introduce new risks, including tunnel and air circulation failures and terrorist attacks. Because they require numerous passengers to travel in enclosed vehicles with limited air circulation, they are likely to have high contagion risks. Tunnel roads may increase total vehicle travel and sprawl, contradicting strategic planning goals.

Roles

If tunnel and pneumatic tube transport are as cost effective, efficient, and safe as proponents claim, they may be suitable for implementation on some travel corridors. If pneumatic tube transport proves to be efficient, public policies may encourage it as a substitute for medium-distance air travel.

Aviation Innovations
(Drones, Air Taxis, and Supersonic Jets)

Aviation innovations include various emerging air travel technologies and services.[136] *Delivery drones* are small, autonomous, electric-powered aircraft suitable for delivering light packages (usually less than ten pounds), with speeds up to 60 miles per hour and ranges up to 50 miles.[137]

Air taxis (also called *sky taxis, urban air mobility* or *flying cars*) are small (two-to-five-passenger), autonomous, electric-powered aircraft capable of vertical takeoff and landing (VTOL).[138] They have speeds up to 180 miles per hour and ranges up to 60 miles.[139]

Supersonic commercial jets can transport people faster than the speed of sound (768 miles per hour) with ranges of 4,000 to 6,000 miles.[140]

Although these modes differ in size, performance, and payload, they all use advanced technologies to provide commercial air travel services.

Current Status

Delivery drones have been used in small-scale pilots, such as the Zipline company's use of drones to deliver medical materials in rural Africa,[141] and Amazon's proposed Prime Air small package delivery service.[142] However, large-scale commercial drone delivery services do not currently exist, and their future potential is uncertain. Most jurisdictions restrict drone operation for safety and security reasons, and there is likely to be public opposition to their use for common commercial deliveries in urban areas.

Optimists predict that air taxis and supersonic commercial jets will soon be commercially available, but these modes require significantly more development, testing, and approval before they can operate in most jurisdictions, and their ultimate performance and profitability are uncertain.[143]

The User Experience

Delivery drones, air taxis, and supersonic jets are likely to be less convenient and comfortable than conventional alternatives. In many situations, sending and receiving drone packages will require more effort (such as somebody available to receive packages) and special infrastructure (such as landing pads) than postal or land-based courier services. Air taxis are likely to be more crowded, noisier, and less comfortable than luxury automobiles, and supersonic jets are likely to be more crowded, noisier, and less comfortable than first-class airline travel.[144]

Travel Impacts

If they operate as proposed, these modes are likely to increase total vehicle travel. Compared with post and courier services, which use vehicles carrying numerous parcels, a drone carrying a single parcel and returning empty generates far more vehicle-miles. Air taxis are likely to encourage longer trips and sprawled development. Because supersonic jets are small, they increase plane travel compared with the same number of passengers on conventional commercial flights.

Benefits and Costs

Aviation innovations can increase travel speeds. Drones can provide fast, direct delivery of small packages. Air taxis can often travel faster and more directly than automobiles, although door-to-door gains are likely to be modest in many situations considering the extra time required to access terminals and destinations. Supersonic jet service can significantly reduce flight durations compared with conventional jets, although door-to-door time savings are more modest. For example, for a typical London-to-New York trip, a supersonic jet can reduce in-air time by about half, from approximately seven hours to three and a half hours, but since it typically takes at least five hours to access a major airport, check in, board, clear customs, and reach a final destination, the door-to-door journey time typically declines from twelve to nine hours, or only 25 percent.

Although their costs are difficult to predict, drones, air taxis, and supersonic jet travel will probably be much more expensive than conventional alternatives. Commercial drone deliveries will probably cost several times more than conventional courier services or post deliveries. Industry advocates optimistically predict that autonomous air taxi fares could be comparable to those of ridehailing or short airplane flights,[145] but even those fares are unaffordable for most commuters, and considering all costs, including terminals, insurance, and profits, actual fares are likely to be higher than these optimistic predictions.[146] Supersonic jets require sophisticated design and construction, require costly maintenance and ground support, are fuel intensive, and carry small passenger loads and minimal freight (airlines earn a significant portion of profits from cargo carried on conventional jets) so their fares will be high. In 2003, Concorde fares from London to New York averaged about $12,000, which was five to ten times higher than business class, suggesting that supersonic travel will only be cost effective for travelers whose time is worth thousands of dollars per hour.[147]

Drones, air taxis, and supersonic jets are likely to impose significant external costs, including noise and crash risk. Drones and air taxi passengers will look down on homes and yards, intruding on residents' privacy. Proponents claim that new technologies can minimize these impacts, but it is worth being skeptical. Although new technologies may reduce some impacts, their external costs will probably still be greater than most alternatives. For example, electric air taxis are likely to consume less energy, produce less noise, and generate less air pollution than helicopters but far more than automobiles, which is the most common alternative for the fifty-to-one-hundred-mile regional trips that air taxis are intended to serve.[148] The European Commission set drone noise standards at a very high eighty-five decibels, equivalent to a flying gasoline lawnmower.[149] Their crash risks are uncertain but certainly not zero. Under most conditions, drone parcel delivery consumes more energy than either diesel or electric truck parcel delivery, and regular postal delivery is even more efficient because it generates no additional vehicle travel.[150] Supersonic jets cause sonic booms that disrupt large areas and generate much greater climate disruption than conventional jets or other travel modes.[151] Air taxis and supersonic jets are likely to increase contagion risk due to their cramped conditions. If widely used, these modes are likely to increase total vehicle travel and sprawl, which contradicts strategic planning goals.

Roles

If they perform as well as proponents predict, delivery drones, air taxis, and supersonic commercial jets might sometimes provide critical services, such as delivering critical equipment and personnel, but these are likely to be rare and not their primary markets, which are to transport consumer goods, commuters, and wealthy travelers. As a result, their use should be restricted to high-value applications.

Mobility Prioritization

Mobility prioritization uses new technologies and services, including innovative travel information,[152] responsive road and parking fees,[153] plus commuter incentives[154] to favor higher-value trips and more efficient modes over less-valuable and less-efficient options. It is a type of transportation demand management (TDM).

Table 5-4 illustrates typical mobility and parking priorities. Active and public transit modes generally have the highest priority because they are resource efficient (they require minimal space and energy), so their use should be encouraged. Commercial and service vehicles can also receive priority due to their high value. Shared vehicles, such as carpools, vanpools, and microtransit, generally have moderate priority because they are more efficient than single-occupant automobiles but less than full-size buses. Mobile billboards and vehicles cruising to avoid parking fees have the lowest priority and so should be discouraged, particularly in congested areas.

Table 5-4 Typical Mobility and Parking Prioritization. Roads and parking facilities should be managed to favor higher-value uses and more resource-efficient modes. This table lists typical priorities.

Mobility Priority	Parking Priority
1. Walking	1. Passenger loading
2. Bicycling	2. Freight loading
3. Public transit	3. Quick errands (less than 30 minutes)
4. Commercial and service vehicles	4. Longer-term errands
5. Shared automobiles (ridesharing)	(more than 30 minutes)
6. Single-occupant vehicles and taxis	5. Commuting
7. Mobile billboards and cruising	6. Residents
to avoid parking fees	7. Long-term storage

Similarly, the most convenient public parking facilities, including curbs, should be prioritized to favor higher-value activities such as passenger and freight loading and quick errands. In busy urban areas, motorists engaged in longer-term errands, commuters, and residents should be encouraged to use less convenient parking facilities.

New technologies can support prioritization. Real-time traffic information systems can help travelers to decide, for example, whether to shift to a less congested time, route, mode, or destination, and whether to choose an expensive but convenient parking space or a cheaper but less convenient alternative. New technologies can also facilitate efficient pricing. New electronic road and parking payment systems are convenient and cost effective, and allow road and parking prices to vary by time, location, and vehicle type, making them more efficient and fair. Commute trip reduction programs can include app-based tracking, games, and rewards that encourage workers to use efficient modes.

Current Status

Many jurisdictions have some mobility prioritization such as bus, HOV, and bike lanes, plus curb space designated for loading, short-term parking, and taxis. A few jurisdictions apply decongestion pricing, with higher tolls and parking fees during peak periods.[155] For example, the I-10 Metro Express Lanes in Los Angeles, the 95 Express Lanes in Miami, the I-405 Express Toll Lanes in Washington State, the I-635 East TEXpress Lanes in Dallas, and the I-77 Express Lanes in Charlotte, North Carolina, all use electric payment systems to collect variable tolls.[156] Singapore, London, Stockholm, and Oslo all have special decongestion tolls for entering the city center.[157] New York City plans to implement daily fees of eight dollars for passenger vehicles and twenty-one dollars for trucks that drive into lower Manhattan during weekdays.[158] Many jurisdictions have other TDM incentives to encourage travelers to choose resource-efficient modes, including commuter trip reduction programs.[159]

The User Experience

Mobility prioritization can affect user experiences in several ways. It favors higher-value trips and more efficient modes, and so directly benefits motorists who are willing to pay for faster travel or more convenient parking, and travelers who already use active, shared, and public transit modes. However, many motorists dislike paying to use previously unpriced roads or feel that road pricing is unfair.[160]

Travel Impacts

Mobility prioritization can cause various travel changes, depending on type and scale. Efficient road and parking fees typically reduce affected vehicle travel by 10 to 30 percent.[161] Bus and HOV lanes can cause travelers to shift from driving alone to sharing vehicles, particularly if implemented as part of an integrated program that includes rideshare and transit service improvements, and TDM incentives.

Benefits and Costs

Mobility prioritization can increase the travel speed and reliability of higher-value travel, such as freight and service vehicles, buses, and important errands, and allow motorists to identify the best travel or parking options for each trip. It tends to reduce total vehicle travel and therefore traffic and parking congestion, infrastructure costs, crashes, and pollution emissions. By charging motorists for the road and parking costs they impose, and improving ridesharing and public transit service efficiency, it tends to support equity goals overall, although these impacts depend on specific factors, such as the quality of travel options, price structures, and how revenues are used.[162] To the degree that it causes shifts from driving to active modes it tends to increase public fitness and health and reduce contagion risks. Shifts to public transit may increase contagion risks. By encouraging automobile travel reductions and reducing automobile parking needs it helps achieve strategic planning goals.

Roles

Mobility prioritization tends to increase overall transportation system efficiency and fairness by favoring higher-value trips and more efficient modes. It supports and is supported by New Mobilities such as active and public transport improvements, ridesharing, and logistical management. It also supports TDM programs.

Logistics Management

Communities need reliable and efficient freight delivery. Freight transport generates approximately 10 percent of total vehicle travel and 30 percent of transportation pollution emissions. It also imposes significant traffic congestion, parking costs, crash risk, and pollution emissions, particularly in dense urban areas.[163] New technologies and services can increase freight delivery efficiency, reducing total vehicle travel and encourage use of resource-efficient modes, such as shifts from truck to rail, from diesel to electric trucks, and from larger to smaller delivery vehicles including electric-assist cargo bikes and delivery carts.[164]

In most urban regions, numerous firms have their own warehouses and delivery fleets. With integrated freight systems, goods are delivered to a central consolidation center (CCC) where loads are organized by destination and delivery requirements, with some goods being delivered directly by truck and others sent to local consolidation centers from which they are distributed by small electric vehicles or electric-assist cargo bikes.[165] This increases efficiency and reduces large truck travel on local streets where their congestion, crash, noise, and pollution costs are most severe.[166] With vehicle travel reductions and efficient management, downtown parking structures can be repurposed as consolidation centers.[167]

Current Status

Although many companies use logistics innovations, such as dispatching software, radio-frequency identification (RFID) tracking, and vehicle monitoring, few communities have integrated logistics management programs that optimize goods distribution, increase efficiency, and minimize traffic impacts.[168] Such programs are currently under development in some urban regions, with significant potential for improvement and expansion. These allow shippers to use the most appropriate option for each delivery, including smaller electric cargo vans and cargo bikes instead of large diesel trucks.[169]

The User Experience

Businesses can directly benefit from better logistics management. For many firms, goods distribution is an ancillary responsibility; they own warehouses and trucks to support core activities such as manufacturing, retail, or farming. This can be inefficient, particularly if their shipping needs fluctuate, forcing companies to maintain more capacity than usually needed in order to serve occasional peaks.

Travel Impacts

Logistics management can reduce freight vehicle travel and shift to smaller vehicles, particularly in urban areas. Comprehensive programs typically reduce freight vehicle mileage by 10 to 30 percent.[170]

Benefits and Costs

Logistics management generally delivers goods as fast as, or faster than, existing distribution systems. By increasing efficiencies, logistics management can reduce costs, providing savings to businesses and consumers. Because freight trucks impose large congestion, infrastructure, crash, noise, and pollution costs, even small travel reductions can provide large community benefits. By reducing total vehicle travel and reducing city center truck traffic, this tends to support strategic planning goals.

To be successful, integrated logistical management requires a high level of cooperation among governments and businesses. Because many of the benefits are external, strong incentives are often required to overcome obstacles to optimal logistical management implementation.

Roles

Logistics management can be implemented in most regions, and it is especially appropriate in major urban centers where there are large benefits from truck traffic reductions. Regional and local governments should develop freight transportation plans to guide logistics management implementation. This process should integrate central consolidation center development into freight infrastructure planning and provide incentives for shippers to use more sustainable vehicles for local deliveries. Innovative technologies and services such as electric delivery vans, cargo bikes, and autonomous freight vehicles should be anticipated and incorporated.

Conclusion

There you are: comprehensive and systematic evaluations of the New Mobilities. This analysis indicates that these new technologies and services are at various stages of development, can affect travel in many ways, tend to have diverse benefits and costs, and can play many different roles in an efficient and equitable transportation system. Which deserve support and encouragement? Under what circumstances should they be encouraged, restricted or priced? The next chapter uses this information to rate and compare the New Mobilities with regard to various goals and perspectives.

Chapter 6

Analysis:
How New Mobilities
Can Achieve Community Goals

In this chapter I rate and compare the New Mobilities using a combination of quantitative analysis and qualitative judgments, based on information from the previous chapters. I analyze each New Mobility using the eight planning goals described in chapter 4: travel time savings, user savings and affordability, public infrastructure savings, congestion reduction, traffic safety, social equity objectives, resource conservation, reduced pollution, public fitness and health, and minimizing contagion risks.

These impacts are diverse. Some are difficult to predict, and others are unsuitable for quantification. As a result, this is a multi-criteria evaluation. Most ratings are categorized as "Large," "Moderate," or "Small," which translates into a seven-point scale from +3 (large positive effect) to -3 (large negative effect), with 0 being neutral or mixed.

These impacts can vary depending on conditions, so the ratings may need to be adjusted to reflect a particular situation or perspective. An impact that I rate "Large" might more appropriately be rated "Medium" or even "Small" in a particular situation or if integrated with other modes or policies. For example, a bikeshare program may support social equity goals if it is designed and located to serve lower-income users, but not if located in affluent areas. Similarly, autonomous vehicle technology may increase affordability if applied to public transit or taxi services, but not if used for personal automobiles. You can adjust these ratings to reflect specific conditions or different assumptions.

Stages of Development

Let's begin by considering New Mobilities' stages of development. Some, such as tunnel roads, pneumatic tube transport, and air taxis, are still in the concept and design phase. It is too early to predict their ultimate costs and benefits. Others, such as autonomous vehicles, microtransit, and supersonic jets, are being implemented as pilot projects. Most others, including electric vehicles, ridehailing, and Mobility as a Service (MaaS), are commercially available but have potential for further development and market expansion. In contrast, personal automobile travel, and therefore the assumption that every adult should own a motor vehicle that is used for most travel, appears to be peaking and is likely to decline in the future as travelers increasingly rely on alternatives. Table 6-1 shows these stages.

Table 6-1 New Mobility Stages of Development. New Mobilities vary in their stages of development. Some are still undergoing design, testing, or approval. Others are commercially available and now in product development and growth stages.

Product Design	Testing & Approval	Product Development & Growth	Declining
• Tunnel roads • Pneumatic tube transport • Air taxis	• Autonomous vehicles • Microtransit • Supersonic jets	• Mobility as a Service • Ridehailing • Micromobilities • Vehicle sharing • Mobility prioritization • Active transport • Telework • Electric vehicles • Transit innovations • Logistics management	• Personal automobile travel

Travel Changes

How will New Mobilities affect travel activity? Will they increase or reduce per capita motor vehicle miles, active travel, and public transit use? This information can help determine a mode's costs and benefits, and whether it supports or contradicts strategic goals such as vehicle travel reduction targets and compact development objectives.

In general, faster and lower-priced modes tend to increase mobility, while slower and more expensive modes tend to reduce it. Standard economic models can help predict the magnitude of these impacts.[1] For example, if an electric vehicle's operating costs are half those of an equivalent fossil fuel vehicle, its annual mileage will typically increase 10 to 30 percent. Conversely, if travelers shift from owning a personal car to using autonomous taxis that eliminate ownership costs but have three times higher operating costs, their average annual mileage is likely to decline by about half.

Table 6-2 summarizes New Mobilities' typical travel impacts, including *direct impacts* if they increase or reduce vehicle travel, *indirect impacts* if they affect vehicle ownership or change development patterns in ways that affect overall travel patterns, and *impact severity* which reflects the degree that they affect travel with particularly large effects, such as urban-peak, heavy vehicle, or air travel.

Table 6-2 Motor Vehicle Travel Impacts. This table summarizes direct and indirect travel impacts, plus the severity of the affected travel costs.

Modes	Direct Impacts	Indirect Impacts	Impact Severity
	Changes in how people travel	*Changes in vehicle ownership and land use patterns*	*Changes in high-impact travel (e.g., urban-peak, heavy vehicle, and air travel)*
Active Travel and Micromobilities	Moderate reduction. Reduces many short vehicle trips.	Large reduction. Supports transit and compact development.	Moderate. Reduces urban vehicle travel.
Vehicle Sharing	Moderate reduction. Reduces automobile travel.	Moderate reduction. Helps reduce vehicle ownership.	Moderate. Reduces urban vehicle travel.
Ridehailing and Microtransit	Moderate increase due to deadheading.	Moderate reduction. Helps reduce vehicle ownership.	Small. Affects normal travel.

Table 6-2 Motor Vehicle Travel Impacts (continued). This table summarizes direct and indirect travel impacts, plus the severity of the affected travel costs.

Modes	Direct Impacts	Indirect Impacts	Impact Severity
	Changes in how people travel	*Changes in vehicle ownership and land use patterns*	*Changes in high-impact travel (e.g., urban-peak, heavy vehicle, and air travel)*
Electric Vehicles	Large increase due to reduced operating costs.	Small increase. Encourages sprawl.	Small. Affects normal travel.
Autonomous Vehicles	Large increase due to increased convenience.	Moderate increase. Encourages sprawl.	Small. Affects normal travel.
Public Transport Innovations	Moderate reduction. Directly reduces some driving.	Large reduction. Encourages compact development.	Moderate. Reduces urban vehicle travel.
Mobility as a Service (Maas)	Small reduction. Helps reduce auto travel.	Small reduction. Helps reduce vehicle ownership.	Moderate. Reduces urban vehicle travel.
Telework	Moderate reduction. Reduces some auto travel.	Moderate increase. Encourages sprawl.	Moderate. Reduces urban travel.
Tunnel Roads and Pneumatic Tubes	Small increase. Tunnel roads encourage driving.	Moderate increase. Encourages sprawl.	Small. Affects normal travel.
Aviation Innovation	Moderate increase. Encourages air travel.	Small increase. Air taxis encourage sprawl.	Large. Affects air travel, which imposes high costs.
Mobility Prioritization	Moderate reduction. Shifts auto to shared modes.	Moderate reduction. Encourages compact development.	Large. Reduces urban vehicle travel.
Logistics Management	Moderate reduction. Reduces urban truck travel.	Moderate reduction. Encourages compact development.	Large. Reduces heavy urban vehicle travel.

Travel Speeds and Time Costs

Increasing travel speed and reliability and reducing travel time costs are important planning goals. Faster travel increases the activities and destinations we can reach within our travel time budgets, and improving travel convenience and comfort can reduce travel time unit costs. New Mobilities can affect speeds and time costs in the following ways:

- **Increase travel speed and reliability.** New Mobilities are sometimes faster or more reliable than alternatives. For example, micromobilities tend to be faster than human-powered scooters and bicycles, carsharing and ridehailing are often faster than public transport, BRT and high-speed rail are faster than conventional bus and train services, air taxis can be faster than driving, and pneumatic tube transport is predicted to be faster than air travel on some routes.
- **Faster connections.** Some New Mobilities create more direct routes or faster connections. For example, tunnel roads, delivery drones, and air taxis can often travel more direct routes than conventional auto travel. Active mode improvements often include pedestrian and bicycle shortcuts, while public transit improvements, MaaS, and logistics management often accelerate intermodal connections.
- **Reduce travel time unit costs.** Some New Mobilities reduce the cost per hour of time devoted to travel. For example, active and public transport improvements, and autonomous vehicle travel, can reduce traveler stress, increase comfort, and allow travelers to be more productive (rest and work) while traveling, which reduces their travel time costs.
- **Favor higher-value travel.** Some New Mobilities favor higher-value trips. For example, mobility prioritization and logistics management can give urgent trips, public transit, and freight vehicles priority in traffic, allowing travelers to save time when it is most important and beneficial.

Table 6-3 summarizes New Mobilities' travel speed and time cost impacts. These impacts tend to vary depending on specific conditions, how impacts are measured, and what is assumed as the alternative. For example, air taxis can have higher travel speeds than automobiles, but their door-to-door time savings may be modest considering the additional time required to travel to and from terminals and board aircraft. As a result, their overall time savings will depend on terminal density and service efficiency.

Table 6-3 Travel Speed and Time Cost Impacts. This table summarizes travel time impacts. Some New Mobilities increase travel speed. Others reduce travel time unit costs.

Modes	Notable Travel Time Impacts
Active Travel and Micromobilities	Provide more direct routes and reduce stress, which reduces unit time costs. Micromobilities are often faster than active modes (e.g., e-bikes are faster than pedal bikes).
Vehicle Sharing	Generally faster than active and public transport but slower than personal automobile travel due to the additional time required to access vehicles.
Ridehailing and Microtransit	Generally faster than active and public transport but slower than personal automobile travel.
Electric Vehicles	No significant impacts.
Autonomous Vehicles	Similar to human-operated vehicles but reduces drivers' travel time unit costs.
Public Transport Innovations	Often increase travel and connection speeds, and by increasing passenger comfort, reduce their unit costs.
Mobility as a Service	Tends to increase the speed of connections between modes.
Telework	Saves travel time, but may require additional time for telecommunications activities, and may stimulate sprawl, which increases travel time indirectly.
Tunnel Roads and Pneumatic Tube Transport	Can increase travel speeds.
Aviation Innovation	Significantly increases in-air speeds of some intercontinental flights, although door-to-door time savings are more modest.
Mobility Prioritization	Increases the speed and reliability of higher-value trips and space-efficient modes.
Logistics Management	Increases freight delivery speeds.

User Savings and Affordability

New Mobilities vary significantly in their user costs and affordability impacts. Active and public transport improvements, vehicle sharing, and MaaS tend to provide large user savings and affordability opportunities. Micromobilities, ridehailing, and telework can provide extra large affordability benefits if designed to accommodate low-income users—for example, if they serve people who lack internet access, smartphones, and credit cards. Mobility prioritization can increase affordability if road pricing revenues are used to improve affordable modes.[2] Electric vehicles have high ownership costs but low operating costs, and so tend to increase affordability if used for carsharing. Autonomous vehicles, tunnel roads, pneumatic tube transport, and aviation innovations are likely to be expensive, so in most cases provide no savings or affordability benefits. Table 6-4 summarizes affordability impacts.

Table 6-4 Affordability Impacts. Some New Mobilities provide significant savings and affordability benefits.

Affordable	*Contingent (Depends)*	*Expensive*
Active and Micromobilities		Electric Vehicles
Vehicle Sharing		Autonomous Vehicles
Microtransit	Ridehailing	Tunnel Roads
Public Transit Innovations	Telework	Pneumatic Tube Transport
Mobility as a Service	Mobility Prioritization	Aviation Innovations

Public Infrastructure and Congestion Costs

Some New Mobilities are space efficient; they require little space per passenger-mile, which minimizes their infrastructure costs and the congestion they impose on other travelers. Active and micromobilities have low infrastructure costs per travel-mile, due to their small size and light weight, and their costs per passenger-year tend to be small due to their low annual mileage. Bicycles and micro modes can delay motor vehicle traffic if they operate in mixed traffic, but these impacts are small if active transportation improvements include separated facilities. Engineering studies indicate that in most cases, shifts from motorized to nonmotorized modes reduce traffic congestion.[3]

Public transit innovations sometimes require expensive infrastructure such as rail lines and bus lanes, but are usually cheaper than expanding urban roads and parking facilities to accommodate the same number of people traveling by automobile.[4] Vehicle sharing, ridehailing, and MaaS can reduce infrastructure and congestion costs by reducing total vehicle ownership and travel. Ridehailing, electric, and autonomous vehicles are likely to increase total vehicle traffic and therefore infrastructure and congestion costs unless implemented with TDM incentives. Tunnel roads, pneumatic tube transport, and aviation innovations require costly infrastructure; their congestion impacts depend on how they are implemented—for example, how travelers access their terminals. Table 6-5 categorizes these effects.

Table 6-5 Infrastructure and Congestion Costs. Some New Mobilities are space efficient, which reduces infrastructure and congestion costs. Others are space intensive and so increase these costs.

Space Efficient	Contingent (Depends)	Space Intensive
Active and Micromobilities		
Public Transit Innovations		
Telework		
Vehicle Sharing	Ridehailing	
Mobility as a Service	Tunnel Roads	
Mobility Prioritization	Pneumatic Tube Transport	Electric Vehicles
Logistics Management	Aviation Innovations	Autonomous Vehicles

Social Equity Impacts

Social equity analysis is important but challenging because there are many possible ways to define and measure these effects,[5] so it is important to use multiple indicators that reflect various impacts and perspectives.[6] New Mobilities can vary significantly in how they affect disadvantaged groups, including people with mobility impairments or lower income, children,[7] women,[8] seniors, pedestrians, and bicyclists, plus racial and ethnic minorities. These groups tend to face disproportionate obstacles and risks when traveling, including inadequate mobility options for non-drivers, excessive financial costs, physical barriers, and threats of violence and harassment.[9] They also tend to bear excessive burdens of transportation external costs including displacement caused by new facilities, difficulty crossing busy roads, crash risks that motorized modes impose on active travelers, and pollution exposure.[10]

Table 6-6 summarizes their effects on four social equity goals: *universal design* (whether they accommodate people with impairments and other special mobility needs), *affordability* (whether they are priced to serve

Table 6-6 Impacts on Four Social Equity Goals. New Mobilities can have various impacts on physically, economically, and socially disadvantaged groups.

	Universal Design	Affordable	Mobility Quality	External Costs
	Mobility for people with impairments and other special needs	*Priced to serve people with low incomes*	*Vulnerable groups' travel comfort and speed*	*Congestion, crash, and pollution imposed on vulnerable groups*
Active Travel and Micromobilities	Large benefit	Large benefit	Large benefit	Large benefit
Vehicle Sharing	Sometimes	Small benefit	Small benefit	Small benefit
Ridehailing and Microtransit	Sometimes	Small benefit	Small benefit	Small benefit
Electric Vehicles	Sometimes	No benefit	No benefit	Moderate benefit
Autonomous Vehicles	Sometimes	No benefit	No benefit	No benefit
Public Transport Innovations	Large benefit	Large benefit	Large benefit	Large benefit
Mobility as a Service (MaaS)	Moderate benefit	Moderate benefit	Moderate benefit	Moderate benefit
Telework	Large benefit	Moderate benefit	Moderate benefit	Small benefit
Tunnel Roads and Pneumatic Tubes	Sometimes	No benefit	Small benefit	Uncertain
Aviation Innovation	Sometimes	No benefit	No benefit	No benefit
Mobility Prioritization	Sometimes	Large benefit	Large benefit	Moderate benefit
Logistics Management	No benefit	No benefit	No benefit	Moderate benefit

people with low incomes), impacts on vulnerable groups' *quality of mobility* (convenience, comfort, and safety of affordable and inclusive modes such as walking, bicycling, and public transit), and minimizing the *external costs* imposed on vulnerable groups, such as displacement, noise, and pollution inflicted on low-income neighborhoods, plus delay and risk that motor vehicle traffic imposes on pedestrians and bicyclists.

Most active and public transport improvements include universal design features, are affordable, improve disadvantaged people's travel comfort and speed, and reduce external costs imposed on vulnerable groups compared with automobile travel. Some shared, ridehailing, electric, and autonomous vehicles incorporate universal design, but they tend to be less affordable. Modes that increase urban vehicle traffic volumes and speeds tend to increase external costs imposed on vulnerable groups such as pedestrians, bicyclists, and urban residents.

These impacts vary depending on conditions and implementation practices. For example, public policies can require ridehailing services to accommodate people with mobility impairments and users who lack smartphones or credit cards. Programs that improve internet access to disadvantaged and isolated groups can make telework more equitable. Unless they are implemented with TDM incentives, electric and autonomous vehicles tend to increase total vehicle traffic and therefore external costs imposed on pedestrians, bicyclists, and urban neighborhoods. Because electric vehicle owners tend to have high incomes, their subsidies are regressive, although electrification can reduce noise and air pollution damages that vehicle traffic imposes on pedestrians, bicyclists, and urban residents.

Health and Safety

New Mobilities can affect public health and safety if they increase physical activity and fitness, improve disadvantaged people's access to healthcare services, or reduce traffic crash risk.[11] Active and public transport improvements tend to support these public health goals. Vehicle sharing, ridehailing, MaaS, and telework tend to improve access to healthcare services and reduce crash risks by reducing total vehicle travel. Advocates claim that autonomous vehicles, tunnel roads, pneumatic tube transport, and aviation innovations will reduce crash risk, but their analysis tends to exaggerate safety benefits by ignoring new risks that these technologies introduce. If they increase total vehicle travel and sprawl, or discourage active

Table 6-7 Health and Safety Impacts. New Mobilities tend to increase public health and safety if they increase physical activity and fitness, improve access to healthcare services, or reduce crash risks.

Increase Health and Safety	Contingent (Depends)	Reduce Health and Safety
Active and Micromobilities		Electric Vehicles
Public Transit Innovations		Autonomous Vehicles
Vehicle Sharing	Ridehailing	Tunnel Roads
Mobility as a Service	Telework	Pneumatic Tube Transport
Logistics Management	Mobility Prioritization	Aviation Innovations

travel, these modes may reduce public health and safety overall.[12] Logistics management can increase fitness if it increases cargo bike use and increase health and safety if it reduces urban truck traffic. Table 6-7 summarizes health and safety impacts.

Contagion Risk

Public health and transportation professional organizations have developed guidelines for evaluating and reducing the contagion risks of various travel modes.[13] The lowest risks are posed by unenclosed modes, such as walking, bicycling, and micromobilities, plus telework.[14] Active transportation improvements, such as expanded sidewalks and paths, further reduce contagion risk by reducing crowding. Private automobiles with a single user have low risk, but most motorists carry passengers at least occasionally, and COVID-19 infection rates tend to be higher in automobile-oriented areas than in walkable urban neighborhoods, indicating that, in practice, automobile travel has moderate to high contagion risk.[15] If they follow recommended passenger spacing and cleaning practices, carsharing and public transit probably also have moderate risk. Public transit improvements that increase vehicle speeds, reduce crowding, improve ventilation, and automate fare payments can reduce contagion risk.[16] Ridehailing, pneumatic tube transport, air taxis, and supersonic jets are likely to have high contagion risk because they carry numerous passengers in crowded, enclosed vehicles for longer duration trips. Table 6-8 summarizes contagion risk impacts.

Table 6-8 Contagion Risk. Contagion risk is low for unenclosed travel and tends to increase with passenger turnover and crowding.

Low Risk	Contingent (Depends)	High Risk
Active and Micromobilities	Carsharing	
Personal Autonomous Vehicles	Public Transit Innovations	Ridehailing
Personal Electric Vehicles	Mobility as a Service	Pneumatic Tube Transport
Telework	Mobility Prioritization	Air Taxis
Drone Delivery	Tunnel Roads	Supersonic Jets

Resource Conservation and Emission Reductions

Some New Mobilities are resource efficient.[17] Active and micromobilities, public transit, MaaS, mobility prioritization, and logistics management tend to reduce resource consumption and pollution emissions compared with conventional automobile travel. Vehicle sharing, ridehailing, and telework can conserve energy and reduce emissions if they reduce total vehicle travel, with additional benefits if they use electric vehicles. Electric vehicles reduce fossil fuel consumption and pollution emission, especially if electricity is generated using renewable sources. However, these benefits may be partly offset if their low operating costs induce additional vehicle travel,

Table 6-9 Resource Conservation and Pollution Emissions. Some New Mobilities are resource efficient or reduce total vehicle travel, which conserves energy and reduces pollution emissions. Some are resource efficient if they use electric vehicles and are implemented with TDM incentives. Pneumatic tube transport is probably more resource efficient than jet travel.

Resource Efficient	Contingent (Depends)	Resource Intensive
Active and Micromobilities		
Public Transit Innovations	Telework	
Electric Vehicles	Vehicle Sharing	
Mobility as a Service	Ridehailing	Tunnel Roads
Mobility Prioritization	Autonomous Vehicles	Air Taxis
Logistics Management	Pneumatic Tube Transport	Supersonic Jets

so they are most beneficial if implemented with TDM incentives and anti-sprawl policies that prevent traffic growth.[18] Tunnel roads, high-speed rail, and pneumatic tube transport facilities have significant embodied energy (energy used to build infrastructure and vehicles), so their life-cycle efficiency depends on the intensity of their use. Supersonic jet travel is energy intensive, and because its emissions occur at high altitudes, causes severe climate damage. Pneumatic tube transport may reduce energy consumption and pollution emissions if it substitutes for jet travel. Table 6-9 summarizes these effects.

Strategic Planning Goals

Many communities have strategic goals to reduce automobile dependency and total vehicle travel, create more compact and multimodal neighborhoods, and reduce impervious surface area (pavement), as discussed in chapter 4. Active and public transport, vehicle sharing, MaaS, mobility prioritization, and logical management tend to support those goals by reducing vehicle ownership and use, and helping to create more compact, livable urban communities. Ridehailing, telework, and pneumatic tube transport are likely to increase vehicle travel and sprawl unless implemented with TDM incentives and Smart Growth policies. Electric and autonomous vehicles, tunnel roads, and aviation innovations tend to contradict strategic goals by increasing total vehicle travel and sprawl. Table 6-10 summarizes impacts on strategic goals.

Table 6-10 Strategic Goals. New Mobilities that reduce total vehicle travel and sprawl help achieve strategic community goals. Those that stimulate vehicle travel and sprawl tend to contradict these goals.

Supports Goals	Contingent (Depends)	Contradicts Goals
Active and Micromobilities		
Public Transit Innovations		
Vehicle Sharing		Electric Vehicles
Mobility as a Service	Ridehailing	Autonomous Vehicles
Mobility Prioritization	Telework	Tunnel Roads
Logistics Management	Pneumatic Tube Transport	Aviation Innovations

Impact Summary

This chapter evaluates twelve New Mobilities according to eight impacts. That's a lot to consider! Table 6-11 summarizes these ratings using a seven-point scale.

Let me highlight some key implications of this analysis.

Active and public transport improvements, along with micromobilities, have the highest total ratings because they provide the greatest variety of benefits. Vehicle sharing, MaaS, mobility prioritization, and logistics management can also provide numerous benefits, but some of these benefits are moderate in magnitude, resulting in somewhat smaller ratings. These modes tend to complement other New Mobilities; for example, public transit improvements become more cost effective and beneficial if

Table 6-11 Summary Table (3 = best; -3 = worst). This table summarizes New Mobilities' ratings against eight impacts.

Modes	Speed & Time	Savings & Affordability	Infrastructure & Congestion	Social Equity	Health & Safety	Contagion Risk	Resources	Strategic Goals	Totals
Active and Micromobilities	1	3	3	3	3	3	3	3	22
Vehicle Sharing	1	2	3	2	2	-2	2	2	12
Ridehailing and Microtransit	1	1	0	1	0	-3	1	1	2
Electric Vehicles	0	0	-3	-2	-3	-1	3	-3	-9
Autonomous Vehicles	3	-2	-3	-1	-2	-1	-3	-3	-12
Public Transit	3	3	2	3	3	-2	3	3	18
Mobility as a Service	2	2	2	2	2	0	2	2	14
Telework	3	2	2	1	0	3	1	-1	11
Tunnels and Pneumatic Tube Transport	2	-3	-2	-3	-2	-3	-2	-3	-16
Aviation Innovation	3	-3	-3	-3	-3	-3	-3	-3	-18
Mobility Prioritization	3	1	3	1	1	0	3	3	15
Logistics Management	2	0	3	1	2	0	3	3	14

implemented with active modes, MaaS, and mobility prioritization, so their total ratings increase if they are implemented as an integrated package.

Ridehailing, microtransit, and telework have positive ratings, but with current policies are likely to increase total vehicle travel and sprawl, which increases many external costs. As a result, their benefits are much larger if implemented with TDM incentives and Smart Growth policies. For example, to prevent ridehailing from increasing urban traffic problems it should be implemented with decongestion pricing, and to prevent telework from increasing sprawl it should be implemented with Smart Growth policies to discourage sprawl.

Private electric and autonomous vehicles, tunnel roads, pneumatic tube transport, and aviation innovations have negative total ratings because they provide a limited variety of benefits, are expensive to own or use, and tend to increase total vehicle travel and external costs. Their ratings increase if they become more affordable and are implemented with TDM incentives and Smart Growth policies to prevent induced travel and sprawl. Electric and autonomous vehicle benefits increase significantly if they are used for carsharing, taxis, transit buses, and local delivery services.

Of course, these impacts can vary significantly depending on conditions, and they may change in the future. For example, because they are space efficient, active and public transport, vehicle sharing, MaaS, mobility prioritization, and logistics management are most beneficial in denser urban areas where congestion and pollution problems are most severe. On the other hand, ridehailing and electric and autonomous vehicles can efficiently serve dispersed destinations, and so are more appropriate in suburban and rural areas. All of these modes become more cost effective and beneficial if implemented with TDM incentives that encourage travelers to choose the most optimal option for each trip, including smaller vehicles for local trips, shared vehicles on busy travel corridors, and telework when possible. These impacts also depend on future technological progress. If autonomous vehicles, delivery drones, air taxis, and supersonic jets become as safe, quiet, affordable, and efficient as optimists predict, their ratings may rise, but planners should be skeptical and demand credible evidence.

Conclusions

This analysis rates and compares New Mobilities according to various impacts and community goals. This can help determine which New Mobilities are most effective at achieving particular goals, which provide the greatest overall benefits, and which policies can help prevent potential problems and maximize their total benefits.

This analysis combines science and art: it uses a multi-criteria evaluation framework that incorporates both quantitative and qualitative information. This allows it to consider impacts that are important but difficult to quantify, and so is more comprehensive than benefit-cost analysis, which only considers impacts that can be monetized (measured in monetary units).

This analysis indicates that active and public transport improvements, and micromobilities, provide the greatest variety of benefits because they are affordable, resource-efficient, and promote good health. Vehicle sharing, ridehailing, MaaS, and telework are somewhat more costly and resource intensive but still provide numerous benefits, particularly if they help reduce total vehicle travel. As a result, their benefits increase if they are implemented as an integrated package with mobility prioritization, TDM incentives, and Smart Growth policies, so they help achieve strategic goals to reduce total vehicle travel and create more compact, multimodal communities.

In contrast, higher-speed modes, including private electric and autonomous vehicles, tunnel roads, pneumatic tube transport, and aviation innovations, provide fewer benefits because they are expensive and resource intensive and tend to impose significant external costs. Because they increase travel speeds, these modes tend to rate well under the old planning paradigm, which focused on increasing mobility and considered a limited set of community goals, but less well under the new paradigm, which focuses on improving overall accessibility and considers a greater variety of community goals.

These impacts can vary depending on conditions and policies. For example, with current policies, electric and autonomous vehicles are likely to induce more vehicle travel and therefore external costs, so their net benefits (benefits minus costs) increase if they are implemented with TDM incentives and Smart Growth policies. Some impacts may change over time. Electric and autonomous vehicles, pneumatic tube transport, and air taxis may become more affordable and efficient over time, in which case their benefits will increase, but this is likely to take decades.

These ratings are my judgments, based on the assumptions and information described in previous chapters. You may disagree with some of my analysis methods and results. For example, this analysis gives equal weight to each of the eight impacts; you may consider some more important than others. Advocates of a particular mode may believe that I underestimate its benefits or overestimate its costs. Similarly, you may believe that I exaggerate demand for certain modes, such as public transit, MaaS, or logistics management, and so think that they deserve lower rankings. Certainly, other conclusions are possible, and I encourage you to test alternative assumptions. However, I doubt that most reasonable adjustments will significantly affect the overall results of the analysis. For example, increasing the weight given to travel time savings cannot offset the fact that higher-speed modes, such as electric and autonomous vehicles, pneumatic tube transport, and supersonic jets, are expensive and resource intensive, involve little physical activity, and are likely to increase total vehicle travel and external costs unless they are implemented with strong TDM incentives and anti-sprawl policies.

These results do not mean that lower-rated modes are bad and should be forbidden, but it does indicate that New Mobilities vary significantly in their net benefits. This analysis indicates which modes provide the greatest overall benefits, and so deserve the most public support. It also indicates that some modes, including ridesharing and electric and autonomous vehicles, should be implemented with TDM incentives and Smart Growth policies to prevent them from increasing total vehicle travel and sprawl. The next chapter provides more specific recommendations for integrating and optimizing the New Mobilities.

Chapter 7

Recommendations for Optimizing New Mobilities

This chapter describes specific ways that communities can implement New Mobility to maximize their benefits and minimize potential problems.

What Others Recommend

Many experts and organizations offer advice for implementing New Mobilities. These vary in perspective and scope. Advocates highlight the benefits of emerging modes, and so recommend their speedy implementation.[1] Skeptics highlight their costs and risks and recommend policies to limit negative impacts.[2] Some try to provide balanced recommendations.[3]

For example, Bruce Schaller's report *The New Automobility* evaluates ridehailing impacts.[4] It concludes that ridehailing can provide significant benefits but warns, "Without public policy intervention, big American cities are likely to be overwhelmed with more automobility, more traffic and less transit and drained of the density and diversity which are indispensable to their economic and social well-being." It recommends policies to prevent ridehailing from increasing traffic problems and inequity.

The National Association of City Transportation Officials' *Guidelines for Regulating Shared Micromobility* recognizes the potential benefits of scooter, bike, and e-bike sharing services, but also various costs and risks they can impose, and so recommends policies to ensure they are used safely and responsibly.[5] These include municipal standards for compliance, equipment, service quality, data integrity, and fleet size, plus regulations and programs to minimize conflicts in public rights-of-way.

Daniel Sperling's book *Three Revolutions* highlights the potential benefits of automated, electric, and shared vehicles but recognizes potential problems if they increase total vehicle travel and sprawl, as well as the need for policies that favor more resource-efficient modes.[6] The National Association of City Transportation Officials' *Blueprint for Autonomous Urbanism* recommends that, to maximize community benefits, autonomous vehicle policies should emphasize safety, maximize person rather than vehicle throughput, and ensure that benefits are distributed equitably.[7] It warns that "automation without a comprehensive overhaul of how our streets are designed, allocated, and shared will not result in substantive safety, sustainability, or equity gains."

Hana Creger, Joel Espino, and Alvaro S. Sanchez's report *Autonomous Vehicle Heaven or Hell? Creating a Transportation Revolution that Benefits All* for the Greenline Institute, an environmental and social equity advocacy organization, concludes that "if left up to the free market without adequate regulation, we can expect a 'hell' scenario dominated by personally-owned autonomous vehicles that are only accessible to those who can afford them, while further congesting our streets and polluting our air, leaving others to cope with worse traffic, longer commutes and under-resourced public transit."[8] To achieve more positive results they recommend policies that favor fleets of autonomous vehicles that are electric and shared (FAVES). Similarly, Tom Cohen and Clémence Cavoli's article "Automated Vehicles: Exploring Possible Consequences of Government (non)intervention for Congestion and Accessibility" argues that laissez-faire free-market policies will cause autonomous vehicles to increase traffic congestion and reduce accessibility for non-drivers, resulting in undesirable outcomes.[9]

Stephen Goldsmith's *Governing* magazine article "An Impact Framework for the New Mobility" recommends that New Mobility planning should consider these impacts:[10]

- *Access and equity:* How do decisions increase or decrease access and for whom, and how do they mitigate or aggravate equity issues?
- *Environment:* How do transportation decisions affect air quality and public health both broadly and within a neighborhood?
- *Sidewalk usage:* How should we allocate valuable curb and sidewalk space?
- *Revenue:* How do decisions regarding parking rates or regulatory fees affect both user behaviors and a city's ability to cross-subsidize other transportation modes?

- *Safety:* How does a decision protect or endanger riders, pedestrians, and bystanders?
- *Privacy:* How should transportation-related data be protected, used, shared, accessed, and stored to maximize both efficiency and privacy?

Figure 7-1 illustrates the *Shared Mobility Principles for Livable Cities*, developed by a consortium of sustainable development advocacy organiza-

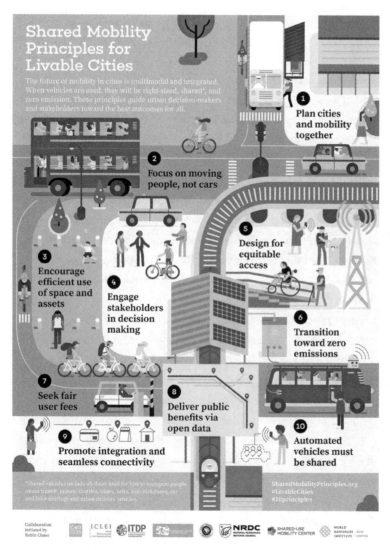

Figure 7-1 Shared Mobility Principles for Livable Cities. (Graphic courtesy of WRI, www.sharedmobilityprinciples.org/resources)

tions, which describe specific principles to ensure that new transportation technologies and services maximize overall efficiency and equity.

Although these documents vary in scope and perspective, they all reach similar conclusions: transportation innovations can provide many benefits but can also impose significant problems and risks, and so must be carefully evaluated and implemented. Box 7-1 distills these recommendations into six key principles.

BOX 7-1 PRINCIPLES FOR EFFICIENT AND EQUITABLE TRANSPORTATION PLANNING

- **Focus on accessibility.** Mobility is seldom an end in itself; the ultimate goal of most travel is to access services and activities. Many factors affect accessibility, including quality of travel by various modes, transport network connectivity, land use density and mix, and mobility substitutes such as telework and delivery services. Optimal planning balances these factors to maximize overall accessibility.
- **Value mobility diversity.** An efficient and equitable transportation system must be diverse to serve diverse demands, including the mobility needs of people who cannot, should not, or prefer not to drive for some or all trips.
- **Encourage resource efficiency.** An efficient transportation system favors resource-efficient modes in planning and management, and encourages travelers to use the most efficient option for each trip.
- **Encourage economic efficiency.** Economic efficiency recognizes that the value of travel can vary, and so favors higher-value trips such as freight and service vehicles and urgent errands, with regulations and efficient pricing.
- **Recognize social equity goals.** Equitable mobility planning means that people are treated fairly and disadvantaged groups are protected. This includes applying universal design (facilities and services that accommodate diverse users, including people with impairments and other special needs); policies that favor affordable and inclusive modes over more expensive, exclusive travel options; and programs that provide basic mobility for disadvantaged groups.
- **Recognize community safety, health, and environmental goals.** Transportation planning decisions affect safety, health, and the environment, and so favor safer, healthier, and less-polluting mobility options.

Integrated Policies and Planning Practices

New Mobility planning requires a foundation of integrated policies and planning practices that facilitate innovation and ensure that the results are efficient and inclusive. Following are specific actions that communities can take to help make this happen.

A Culture of Innovation

For optimal implementation, New Mobilities require that communities and planning organizations encourage innovation. This involves a tolerance for uncertainty, risk taking, and failure.[11] It also requires stakeholder and community engagement in order to identify and address potential problems that develop. Of course, a culture of innovation should not assume that newer is always better; on the contrary, it requires critical and comprehensive analysis of short- and long-term impacts.

Proactive Planning

Some jurisdictions are starting to develop strategic planning programs to prepare for emerging transportation technologies and services.[12] Following are three examples.

- The City of Seattle's *New Mobility Playbook* offers guidelines for implementing a broad variety of emerging technologies, including vehicle sharing, ridehailing, MaaS, and electric and autonomous vehicles.[13] It starts by reviewing the city's strategic goals that should be considered with evaluating specific policies, including safety, connectivity, vibrancy, affordability, and innovation. It critically examines how new mobilities can support or contradict those goals, defines new mobility principles, and identifies specific near-term policies that the city should implement to ensure that new mobilities support the city's goals.
- The Los Angeles Department of Transportation's *Transportation Technology Action Plan* recognizes that "code is the new concrete," and asks, "How do we focus on Transportation Happiness and Universal Basic Mobility with the same intensity as we have traditionally focused on moving cars and people faster?"[14] It discusses the types of digital infrastructure that will be needed to support transportation innovations, and discusses issues such as data sharing, privacy, community outreach, and culture change.

- The Denver region's *2030 Mobility Choice Blueprint* discusses the region's growing transportation problems and potential benefits that can be achieved by taking a proactive approach to planning new transportation technologies.[15] It defines various planning objectives (regional collaboration, system optimization, shared mobility, data security and sharing, mobility electrification, driverless vehicle preparation, and new transportation funding), describes how various regional organizations can collaborate to support these objectives, and identifies specific tactical actions to support this process.

Because these issues are emerging and evolving, this planning must be dynamic and responsive, establishing a foundation that will grow and changes with new technologies, problems, and solutions.

Regulatory Reviews

Many existing regulations are outdated and unintentionally limit New Mobility implementation. Regulations concerning sidewalk and path use, taxi operation, vehicle rentals, parking requirements, curb use, home offices, and drone operation should be reviewed and updated to reflect New Mobility needs and impacts.[16] For example, the National Association of City Transportation Officials' *Guidelines for the Regulation and Management of Shared Active Transportation* describes why and how local governments should regulate public sidewalks, paths, and roads to accommodate diverse users and uses; how to adjust parking requirements and management practices to accommodate new modes; recommended business regulations and data reporting requirements for shared vehicle services; plus strategies to achieve social equity goals.[17]

Most taxi regulations require updating to accommodate new technologies and services such as smartphone apps, ridehailing, and Mobility as a Service in order to better support community goals including affordability, social equity, and environmental protection. For example, regulations can require that taxi and ridehailing services accommodate wheelchair users and use hybrid or electric vehicles.

Transportation Demand Management (TDM)

Transportation demand management (TDM) refers to policies and programs that encourage more efficient travel activity.[18] It includes improve-

Table 7-1 Transportation Demand Management Strategies[i]. Transportation demand management includes many policies and programs that encourage more efficient and equitable transportation patterns. They tend to support, and are supported by, New Mobilities.

Improves Transport Options	Incentives to Use Efficient Options	Smart Growth Development Policies	Implementation Programs
• Active transport (walking and bicycling) improvements • Public transit improvements • Rideshare programs • Taxi and ridehailing support • Car- and bikesharing • Guaranteed ride home • Closer commuting • Telework and flextime	• Commuter financial incentives (parking cash-out, transit subsidies, etc.) • Efficient parking pricing • Parking regulations • Efficient road pricing • High-occupancy vehicle priority • Fuel and carbon taxes • Vehicle taxes and fees • Distance-based pricing	• Complete streets policies • Smart Growth/ New Urbanism • Transit-oriented development (TOD) • Location-efficient development • Reduced parking minimums • Efficient parking management • Traffic calming	• Commute trip reduction programs • Freight transport management • Mobility management marketing • School and campus transport management • Tourist transport management • Transport planning reforms

[i] VTPI (2020). "Online TDM Encyclopedia." Victoria Transport Policy Institute, www.vtpi.org /tdm; Randy Machemehl, et al. (2013). *Travel Demand Management Guidebook*. TxDOT Project 6-0702, Center for Transportation Research, University of Texas at Austin https://library.ctr.utexas .edu/ctr-publications/6-0702-p2.pdf.

ments to resource-efficient modes, incentives for travelers to choose the most efficient option for each trip, Smart Growth development policies, multimodal communities, and various targeted programs, as summarized in Table 7-1. TDM is often more cost effective and beneficial than conventional solutions such as road and parking facility expansions, considering all impacts.[19]

Many communities around the world are implementing TDM to address specific problems such as traffic congestion, parking problems, and pollution emissions.[20] The Texas A&M Transportation Institute developed a *How to Fix Congestion* website that includes guidance on the implementation of many TDM strategies,[21] and the City of San Francisco's TDM program includes a *TDM Planning Tool* that provides step-by-step instructions for creating a TDM Plan.[22] Highway advocates sometimes claim that TDM has been tried but failed, citing, for example, unsuccessful carpool or transit promotion campaigns, but integrated TDM programs that are implemented with adequate support have proven successful and cost effective.[23] For example, Washington State's Commute Trip Reduction law, which requires large employers to encourage their workers to use resource-efficient modes, has been renewed by the state since 1991, with business community support, due to its demonstrated effectiveness.[24]

One TDM strategy, called *mobility management marketing*, encourages travelers to try new, resource-efficient travel options.[25] The City of Portland's SmartTrips program, which used individualized marketing to encourage residents to drive less and rely more on other modes, caused 8 to 12 percent reductions in automobile trips, with impacts that lasted at least two years.[26] Such programs are most effective if implemented in conjunction with active and public transport improvements—for example, after completing a bike network or public transit service improvement.

TDM encourages use of resource-efficient New Mobilities such as active and public transport, micromobilities, vehicle sharing, MaaS, mobility prioritization, and logistics management. It can also prevent ridehailing, electric, and autonomous vehicles from increasing total vehicle travel and associated traffic problems.[27]

Vehicle Travel Reduction Targets

During the last century, various transportation policies favored automobile travel to the detriment of other modes.[28] In order to guide multimodal planning and TDM policies, many jurisdictions have established vehicle travel reduction targets.[29] For example, California Senate Bill 743 requires that transportation and land use planning decisions support the state's goal to reduce per capita vehicle travel 15 percent by 2050,[30] Similarly, Washington State legislation directs planning decisions to support a 50 percent reduction in per capita vehicle mileage by 2050.[31] Many local governments also have vehicle travel reduction policies and targets.[32] Such policies lead to greater consistency between different jurisdictions and agencies—for example, encouraging state departments of transportation to support more multimodal planning, with more investments in HOV lanes, public transit, and active travel, and for local governments to implement Smart Growth development policies to create more walkable,

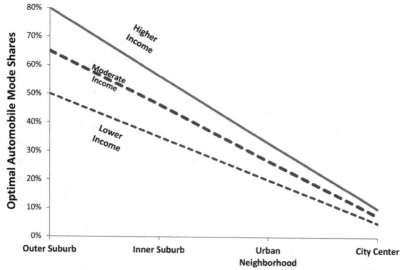

Figure 7-2 Optimal Automobile Mode Shares by Location and Income. Optimal automobile mode shares decline with density and poverty. To maximize efficiency and equity, urban areas need multimodal transportation systems. New Mobilities can help achieve these objectives. (Todd Litman [2017]. "Determining Optimal Urban Expansion, Population and Vehicle Density, and Housing Types for Rapidly Growing Cities." *Transportation Research Procedia*, 2015 World Conference on Transport Research, www.vtpi.org/WCTR_OC.pdf.)

bikeable, and transit-oriented neighborhoods.[33] Vehicle travel reduction targets should reflect geographic and economic factors, with lower automobile mode shares in denser and lower-income communities where there is more demand for non-auto modes, and more benefits from reducing automobile traffic, as illustrated in Figure 7-2.

Transportation Pricing Reforms

New Mobilities can benefit from transportation pricing reforms. As discussed in chapter 3, efficiency and equity require that, as much as possible, travelers pay directly rather than indirectly for the facilities and services they use, with prices that reflect the costs that a vehicle imposes—for example, with higher rates for driving under congested conditions and for larger or more polluting vehicles. Transportation pricing reforms include fuel tax increases and carbon pricing,[34] efficient road[35] and parking pricing,[36] plus distance-based vehicle taxes, registration fees, and insurance premiums.[37] These give travelers incentive to use resource-efficient travel options, including electric rather than fossil fuel vehicles, shifts from peak to off-peak travel times, and shifts to resource-efficient modes that reduce congestion and pollution costs imposed on other people.

These pricing reforms can increase affordability by giving travelers new opportunities to save money when they choose more resource-efficient travel options. For example, current parking policies force people to pay for parking facilities through taxes and rents, regardless of how many vehicles they own and how much they drive. With efficient parking pricing, users pay for parking directly, so households can save money if they reduce their vehicle ownership, drive less, or choose cheaper parking facilities. This rewards travelers who use resource-efficient New Mobilities, such as micro modes and shared vehicles. Since automobile ownership and use tend to increase with income, efficient pricing tends to be progressive with respect to income—it reduces cost burdens on lower-income, car-free households.

These pricing reforms support New Mobilities when they are appropriate and beneficial, and prevent them from being used inefficiently. For example, fuel tax increases encourage motorists to shift from fossil fuel to electric vehicles, and efficient road tolls discourage users from programming their autonomous vehicles to drive around in circles, increasing traffic congestion, crash risk, and pollution, in order to avoid paying for off-street parking. Similarly, efficient fuel and road pricing encourages commuters to use resource-efficient modes, and shippers to use more efficient freight distribution systems and resource-efficient vehicles—such as small electric delivery vans and cargo bikes—instead of full-size trucks, in urban areas.

Planning and Funding Reforms

New Mobilities often benefit from planning and funding reforms that allow investments in new transportation technologies and services. Most jurisdictions have dedicated funds for roads and parking facilities but fewer funding options for other modes and TDM programs, even if they are better investments, considering all benefits and costs. These existing planning and funding practices tend to underinvest in New Mobilities, particularly those that help achieve emerging planning goals such as affordability, social equity, or public health. One reform, called *least-cost transportation planning*, allows funding to be invested in the modes or projects that are most cost effective overall, considering all impacts.[38] This tends to increase support for many New Mobilities, particularly those that help achieve emerging planning goals. For example, with least-cost planning, transportation agencies can shift funds that would otherwise be dedicated to roadway and parking facility expansions to instead improve resource-efficient modes, or to support TDM programs that encourage users to choose resource-efficient travel options.

For example, with least-cost planning, a state or regional transportation agency would compare the benefits and costs of a highway expansion with alternatives, which could include various combinations of public transit improvements, mobility prioritization (such as high-occupancy vehicle lanes or decongestion pricing), and commute trip reduction programs. A local transportation agency would compare the total value of a local arterial expansion with alternatives that could include various combinations of active and public transport improvements, vehicle sharing programs, mobility prioritization, plus TDM incentives such as commute trip reduction and efficient parking pricing. If a local school experiences traffic and parking congestion problems, school and local planners would compare the benefits and costs of road and parking lot expansions with a combination of local pedestrian and bicycling improvements, traffic management, and school transport management programs that reduce the portion of students driven to school. Similarly, a transit agency would compare bus service expansions with contracted microtransit or ride-hailing services.[39] All of these options should be evaluated based not only on their effectiveness at reducing congestion but also on their ability to achieve other planning goals such as increasing affordability, providing independent mobility for non-drivers, improving public fitness and health, and supporting more compact development.

Similarly, money that is currently dedicated to parking facilities can sometimes be reinvested in New Mobilities. Local governments can reduce parking minimums if developers finance on-site bikesharing or carsharing or subsidize public transit or ridehailing services.[40] Many transit agencies subsidize expensive park-and-ride facilities. These funds can instead be used to support bikesharing, micro modes, ridehailing, and microtransit services that provide last-mile services.

Many New Mobilities, such as public transit innovations, MaaS, telework, and logistics management, increase transportation system efficiency, and so are particularly effective at achieving regional congestion reduction and air quality goals. These tend to have synergistic effectives: they become more effective and beneficial if implemented as an integrated program that includes mobility prioritization and other TDM incentives.

As discussed in chapter 4, when evaluating transportation policies and programs, it is generally best to measure impacts *per capita annual*, so they can be compared with other government and household expenditures.

For example, the US Federal Highway Administration's Nonmotorized Transportation Pilot Program spent about $89 million to improve walking and bicycling conditions in four typical communities.[41] The program caused walking mode share to increase 1.8 points, bicycling mode share to increase 0.4 points, and driving mode share to decrease 2.5 points. Described that way, the program may seem costly and ineffective. However, it could also be described as costing about $22 annually per capita over the program's four years, which is small compared with approximately $800 per capita that governments spend each year on roadways, more than $2,500 per capita annual expenditures on off-street parking facilities, or approximately $5,000 that an average motorist spends each year on their vehicle.[42] The program increased walking trips by 23 percent and bicycling trips by 48 percent and reduced automobile mode share by 2.5 percentage points. If these vehicle travel reductions cause proportional cost savings, the $25 annual investment provided more than $200 annual savings per capita, indicating that each dollar invested in the program delivers more than eight dollars in annual infrastructure and vehicle cost savings. Studies that also account for public health and environmental benefits indicate even larger net benefits, which can justify even greater active mode investments.[43]

Similarly, public transit projects, such as new rail lines or bus lanes, often seem expensive if measured per route-mile, and compared with just the cost of a highway lane, but are usually cheaper than the full costs of accommodating additional automobile trips on the same travel corridor, including vehicle ownership and operating expenses, and the costs of providing parking at destinations.[44] Comparisons between highway and public transit projects should consider additional planning goals, such as affordability, independent mobility for non-drivers, plus support for compact and multimodal development.[45] The costs of public transit that serve non-drivers should be compared with the costs of taxis, ridehailing, or chauffeuring.

For equity analysis, external costs and subsidies should generally be measured annual per capita, so that each person can receive a comparable share of public resources. This means, for example, that if motorists travel on average four times more passenger-miles than transit users (say, 10,000 compared with 2,500 annual passenger-miles), it would be fair to subsidize transit travel four times as much per passenger-mile, so both receive comparable annual public benefits. Of course, higher annual subsidies may be justified for physically or economically disadvantaged travelers, which could justify, for example, wheelchair lifts and costly demand response services to accommodate transit passengers with disabilities, fare discounts or exemptions for low-income transit users, or discounted tolls and parking fees for low-income motorists.

Least-cost planning tends to support investments in New Mobilities that are resource efficient and minimize per capita vehicle travel, and therefore minimize per capita annual external costs. However, these modes generally lack the types of dedicated funding that are available for roads and parking facilities. As a result, to be implemented to the degree that is justified by their benefits, New Mobilities may require new funding sources. Table 7-2 identifies potential options.

Table 7-2 Potential Funding Options for New Mobilities[i]. This table describes some potential funding options for new transportation modes and services.

Name	Description	Advantages	Disadvantages
Discounted bulk fares	Discounted fares for groups such as students or employees.	Increases revenue and transit ridership.	May provide little net revenue.
Property taxes	Increase local property taxes.	Widely applied. Distributes burden widely.	Supports no other objectives. Is considered regressive.
Sales taxes	A special dedicated sales tax.	Distributes burden widely.	Supports no other objectives. Is regressive.
Income tax	Special income tax to fund mobility services.	Progressive with respect to income. Relatively stable.	Difficult to implement.
Fuel taxes	An additional fuel tax.	Widely applied. Reduces vehicle traffic and fuel use.	Is considered regressive.
Vehicle fees	An additional fee for vehicles registered in the region.	Charges motorists for using roadways.	Does not affect vehicle use.
Employee levy	A levy on employees in a designated area or jurisdiction.	Charges for commuters.	Administrative costs. Encourages sprawl if only applied in city centers.
Road tolls	Tolls on some roads or bridges.	Reduces congestion and other traffic problems.	Costly to implement.
Vehicle-miles tax	Distance-based fees on vehicles registered in the region.	Reduces vehicle traffic.	Costly to implement.

Table 7-2 Potential Funding Options for New Mobilities[i] (continued). This table describes some potential funding options for new transportation modes and services.

Name	Description	Advantages	Disadvantages
Parking sales taxes	Special tax on commercial parking transactions.	Is already applied in many cities.	Discourages parking pricing and downtown development.
Parking levy	Special property tax on parking spaces throughout the region.	Large potential. Distributes burden widely. Supports strategic goals.	Costly to implement.
Expanded parking pricing	Increase when and where public parking (e.g., on street) is priced.	Moderate potential. Distributes burden widely. Reduces parking and traffic problems.	Requires parking meters and enforcement.
Development or transport impact fees	A fee on new development to help finance infrastructure, including mobility services.	Charges beneficiaries.	Limited potential.
Land value capture	Special taxes on property that benefits from mobility services.	Large potential. Charges beneficiaries.	May be costly to implement. May discourage infill development.
Advertising	Additional advertising on vehicles and terminals.	Widely used.	Limited potential. Sometimes unattractive.

[i] Todd Litman (2014). "Evaluating Public Transportation Local Funding Options." *Journal of Public Transportation*, 17(1), pp. 43–74, www.vtpi.org/tranfund.pdf.

Road, Curb, and Parking Policy Reforms

Roads, curbs, and parking facilities are valuable and scarce resources. These facilities can be managed to better accommodate new modes and favor higher-value uses.[46] *Complete streets* refers to roadway design and operating practices intended to safely accommodate diverse users and activities.[47] This recognizes that roadways serve diverse modes and functions, including active and public transport, automobile travel and parking, plus social activities such as conversing with neighbors and commercial activities such as sidewalk cafes. All of these uses should be balanced in roadway design and management.[48] Complete streets policies tend to support many New Mobilities, including active and public transport, vehicle sharing, mobility prioritization, and logistics management.

Efficient curb management generally means that passenger and freight loading are prioritized over general metered parking, metered parking is prioritized over unpriced parking, and shorter-term users are prioritized over longer-term users.[49] For example, the City of Seattle has designated some curbs lane as "flex zones," with regulations that favor higher-value uses such as deliveries, passenger loading, and quick errands over lower-value uses such as longer-term parking.[50] Similarly, many jurisdictions are starting to use regulations or pricing to discourage motor vehicle traffic (particularly large trucks), and favor resource-efficient modes or alternative fuel vehicles, particularly in central city neighborhoods.[51] These policies tend to favor resource-efficient New Mobilities such as active travel, micromobilities, shared vehicles, public transit, mobility prioritization, and logistics management.[52]

Since many New Mobilities reduce parking demand, their benefits increase if communities eliminate parking minimums so car-free households are no longer required to pay for costly parking facilities they don't need.[53] As much as possible, parking facility costs should be paid directly by users, which provides large financial incentives to reduce automobile ownership and use. For example, with free parking, commuting by car generally seems cheaper than public transit, because fuel costs are generally lower than transit fares. However, if commuters pay directly for parking, or their parking is *cashed out* (non-drivers receive the cash equivalent of the parking subsidies provided to motorists), they have a much greater incentive to use resource-efficient modes, reducing total parking costs, congestion, crash risk, and pollution emissions. As a result, many North American cities are reducing or eliminating parking minimums,[54] and using innovative management strategies to more efficiently serve parking demands so fewer spaces are needed to meet motorists' needs.[55] For example, in 2017, Buffalo, New York, eliminated minimum parking requirements citywide and replaced them with a requirement for developers to establish transportation demand management plans.[56] Seattle, Washington's Right Size Parking Project developed practical tools for more accurately calculating parking demand in multifamily residential buildings, taking into account geographic and economic factors.[57]

Data Collection and Privacy Concerns

Many New Mobilities use and generate new types of travel data. This can be a valuable public resource, but it can also raise privacy concerns. To maximize value and minimize problems governments should establish comprehensive data collection and reporting requirements for these modes. For example, bike- and carsharing, taxi, ridehailing, and micro-taxi services should be required to report their passenger trips, vehicle travel speeds, revenues, and safety incidents (crashes, near crashes, crimes, and threats). Similarly, autonomous vehicles, pneumatic tube transport, delivery drones, and air taxis should also report travel activities and safety incidents.[58] These systems should be designed and managed to protect privacy—for example, by limiting the amount of personalized information collected and ensuring that the data are protected and are not sold or abused.[59] A good example is the Los Angeles Transportation Technology Action Plan that includes Mobility Data Specification (MDS), which defines the data that transportation services must provide and how it should be managed.[60]

Recommendations for Individual New Mobilities

Following are specific policy prescriptions for maximizing the benefits of individual New Mobilities.

Active Travel and Micromobilities

Communities have many reasons to encourage active and micro modes.[61] They provide efficient, affordable, and healthy mobility, and they support other New Mobilities—for example, by providing access to public transit and shared vehicle services. Demand for these modes, and the benefits they provide, tend to be particularly large in denser and lower-income areas.[62]

Communities should establish targets for improving active travel conditions, using quantitative indicators such as walking and bicycling level-of-service ratings, and increasing active travel, using indicators such as annual active mode miles and minutes of travel, and active mode shares (the portion of trips made by walking and bicycling). Pedestrian and bicycle plans can identify obstacles to active travel—for example, by mapping streets that have inadequate sidewalks or poor bicycling conditions.[63] This information can be used to identify and prioritize active transportation improvements. For example, Portland, Oregon, established specific targets for expanding the city's sidewalk and bikeway networks in order to achieve 7 percent walk and 15 percent bike mode shares by 2035.[64]

Communities should adopt complete streets policies to ensure that all roads accommodate diverse users and uses. Community planning can encourage more compact and mixed development, to create fifteen-minute neighborhoods, as well as more connected roadways with pedestrian and bicycle shortcuts, so most local destinations are easy to access by active modes.[65] Sidewalk and path improvements can improve active travel and can prevent conflicts.[66] For example, the City of Paris is building 650 kilometers of bicycle lanes, much of which was previously vehicle parking lanes, as part of its long-term plan to improve walking and bicycling conditions and reduce automobile traffic.[67]

Active mode improvement programs should receive a fair share of transportation budgets based on comprehensive benefit analysis, or equal to their mode share targets. For example, if a community wants 20 percent of local trips made by walking and bicycling sometime in the future, it should be willing to spend up to this portion of transportation funds to improve those modes.[68]

Micromobilities deliver most of the benefits provided by active modes and, because they can be faster and carry heavier loads, they have the ability to serve more areas and trips. However, they can create new problems, including conflicts with other modes on sidewalks and paths.[69] Where this occurs, jurisdictions should develop appropriate regulations and education programs that define where these modes should operate and park, their maximum speed, and under which circumstances they are required to yield to other facility users.[70]

Because unenclosed travel has the least contagion risk, active travel and micromobility improvements are particularly appropriate during pandemics.[71] This should include efforts to improve and support active travel and recreation, with adequate traffic safety and contagion-prevention design features in public streets, paths, and parks. During the 2020 COVID-19 pandemic, for example, numerous communities implemented pedestrian and bicycle improvements, such as wider sidewalks and pedestrianized streets. In addition, many cities are converting street and parking spaces into walking, shopping, and dining uses in order to reduce crowding and support local businesses.[72] Because of their benefits, many of these are likely to become permanent.

Vehicle Sharing

Public policies should favor shared over privately owned vehicles due to their efficiency and affordability.[73] Shared vehicles can be given preferred use of public parking facilities. Parking minimums can be reduced significantly in buildings with on-site or nearby vehicle sharing services. In a typical situation developers can reduce ten to twenty parking spaces for each on-site carshare vehicle.[74] Local governments can support mobility sharing services with partnerships and incentives.[75] Public transit agencies can support scooter-, bike-, and carshare services at transit stations as part of integrated Mobility as a Service programs.[76]

The Shared Use Mobility Center's report *Equity and Shared Mobility Services* recommends that, to achieve social equity goals, vehicle sharing programs be designed to meet the needs of disadvantaged groups.[77] This can include locating vehicle sharing services in disadvantaged neighborhoods, and providing information and payment options for users who lack smartphones and credit cards, targeted outreach and education programs, plus need-based discounts. For example, the nonprofit Ithaca Carshare used a federal grant to offer an Easy Access program that waived application fees, allowed fees to be paid in cash, and offered a fifteen-dollar monthly driving credit.

Bike- and micromobility sharing can serve many short trips, and so should be encouraged, particularly in dense urban areas. Many cities are implementing shared micromobility programs.[78] Their success varies depending on local conditions and support.[79] Between 2010 and 2020, many cities established docked pedal bikesharing, some of which transitioned to dockless bikesharing, and many subsequently to e-scooter and e-bike sharing.[80]

To be successful, these programs require suitable facilities, including sidewalks and paths, and management programs to minimize problems such as conflicts with other sidewalk and path users, and inappropriately parked scooters and bikes.[81] To provide high-quality service that attracts users and maximizes benefits, these services may require direct or indirect subsidies, such as program funding or free parking. Because they are unenclosed, shared micromobility has low contagion risk, and so these improvements and encouragement programs can be implemented during pandemics.[82]

Shared micromobility services can be designed to achieve equity objectives. For example, the Chicago region's Divvy for Everyone program offers special services, pricing, and outreach that has increased use by minority and lower-income groups.[83] In 2018, Portland, Oregon, implemented a four-month pilot program to assess the feasibility, safety, and mobility of e-scooters. The experience indicated that scooters could be a positive addition to the city's transportation network, so the program was improved and expanded.[84]

Ridehailing and Microtransit

Ridehailing and microtransit can provide convenient mobility for some types of trips, but they require strategic planning and regulations to minimize potential problems, including increased traffic congestion and re-duced transit ridership. Governments should review taxi and ridehailing regulations to ensure that they can accommodate new technologies and services and help achieve community goals such as safety, affordability, social equity, resource efficiency and fair labor practices.[85] Ridehailing regulations can establish vehicle and driver safety standards, requirements to accommodate passengers with disabilities, fare structures, vehicle type (such as using low-emission vehicles), and data reporting, plus policies regulating use of traffic lanes and curbs.[86] In large cities, ridehailing should be implemented with policies that favor shared vehicles and limit traffic growth,[87] including high-occupancy vehicle (HOV) priority lanes, decon-gestion pricing (tolls on congested roads), efficient curb and parking man-agement,[88] and integration with Mobility as a Service programs.[89]

Microtransit may be useful in situations where conventional public transit is inefficient but should be regulated to prevent private services from displacing public transit on profitable routes, which can cause tran-sit agencies to lose ridership and revenue, leading to reduced service.[90] Communities should reform taxi regulations to encourage competition, innovation, and fair labor practices and develop ridehailing regulations that ensure the services are safe, efficient, and equitable.

Many jurisdictions are developing ridehailing policies.[91] For example, after extensive research and public consultation, the Province of British Columbia established general rules regarding ridehailing insurance and operator requirements, and the City of Vancouver established specific business licensing, fees, and operating rules to integrate ridehailing with existing taxi services.[92]

Electric Vehicles

Because of their environmental benefits, electric vehicles should be en-couraged, particularly for high-mileage vehicles such as taxis, buses, ser-vice vehicles, and freight trucks.[93] Electric-motor scooters and motorcycles should be encouraged, particularly in developing countries where they are common.[94] Governments should help develop public charging stations and require that parking garages be wired to accommodate personal re-chargers. Governments can also purchase electric vehicles for their own fleets.

Electric vehicle subsidies are expensive (compared with other emis-sion reduction strategies) and regressive, and their benefits decline if they increase total vehicle travel and sprawl.[95] Subsidies may be justified in the short term, to stimulate markets, but should be reduced as the technology develops.[96] Electric vehicle emission reduction benefits are too small to justify the use of HOV lanes or exemptions from road user charges and parking fees. The best way to encourage electric vehicle use is to increase fuel and carbon taxes so they become more affordable compared with driving fossil fuel vehicles.

Many governments have electric vehicle encouragement policies. For example, the City of Toronto, Canada, has an Electric Vehicle Strategy that establishes goals that the portion of electric vehicles in the city will increase to 20 percent by 2030 and 80 percent by 2040.[97] To accomplish this the city plans to develop charging infrastructure, provide information and incentives to encourage motorists to choose electric vehicles, promote shared electric vehicles, and use electric vehicles in its operations. To make electric vehicle subsidies more equitable, some jurisdictions, including Connecticut and Oregon, offer income-based electric vehicle supplements and rebates for e-bikes.[98]

Autonomous Vehicles

Autonomous vehicle technologies can provide many benefits, but they can also introduce new problems and risks. For the foreseeable future, while the technology is developing, autonomous vehicles are likely to cause traffic delays if they frequently stop to await human instructions, and they may increase traffic risks.[99] Unless implemented with strong TDM incentives, they are likely to increase total vehicle travel and associated external costs.

Governments and professional organizations should define performance and data reporting standards that autonomous vehicles must meet to legally operate on public roads, including comprehensive data on near and actual collisions.[100] Autonomous vehicle development should focus on shared and commercial vehicle applications, including microtransit, buses, and trucks.[101] Public policies should ensure that autonomous vehicles are programmed to minimize external costs—for example, to avoid traffic delays and risks to other road users, particularly pedestrians and bicyclists. Policies should prevent autonomous technologies from increasing total traffic problems by implementing mobility prioritization, vehicle travel reduction, and anti-sprawl policies, including high-occupancy vehicle lanes, decongestion pricing, and curb management policies, particularly in dense urban areas.[102] Cities should discourage autonomous vehicle users from programming their vehicles to drive in circles or drive home empty in order to avoid paying for parking. As autonomous vehicles become more affordable and common, governments will need to decide under what cir-

Table 7-3 Recommended Autonomous Vehicle Policies. These policies can help ensure that autonomous vehicles maximize benefits and minimize problems.

Professional Organizations	Federal and State	Local
• Establish performance and safety standards. • Establish guidelines for programing autonomous vehicles to minimize delay and risk to other road users. • Identify ways to favor fleet uses, including taxis, buses and freight vehicles.	• Define under what circumstances vehicles may operate without drivers. • Establish testing, reporting, and privacy requirements. • Allow road pricing and regulations to limit vehicle traffic increases.	• Establish vehicle travel reduction targets and programs. • Establish policies that prevent autonomous vehicles from driving in circles to avoid paying parking fees. • Manage roads and curbs to favor shared over private vehicle travel. • Establish vehicle travel reduction targets and programs.

cumstances traffic lanes should be dedicated for their use to allow platooning and, if so, the regulations and fees that will be imposed.

As of 2019, thirty-seven states have adopted autonomous vehicle policies and regulations.[103] These range from the authorization of studies, testing, and reporting requirements to regulations regarding the conditions under which vehicles may operate without a human driver. Some states prevent local governments from banning or regulating autonomous vehicles within their jurisdiction, while Massachusetts requires that autonomous vehicle test projects must receive local government approval. Table 7-3 describes various policies for optimizing autonomous vehicles.

Public Transit Innovations

Because public transit is resource efficient, inclusive, affordable, and provides a catalyst for more compact and multimodal development, it can help achieve many community goals. It therefore deserves support to improve service and encourage ridership. Public transit innovations can include various new technologies and facility improvements such as navigation apps and automated fare payment systems,[104] dedicated bus lanes, transit priority control systems,[105] more comfortable stops and stations, transit-oriented development,[106] and amenities such as on-board Wi-Fi.[107] Public transit innovations can integrate with other New Mobilities including active and micro modes, vehicle sharing, MaaS, and mobility prioritization. Ridehailing can provide last-mile access to public transit services, increasing their efficiency, but should be regulated and priced to limit low-occupancy trips on busy urban corridors, so it does not displace high-volume public transit service.[108] To maximize the effectiveness and benefits of public transit innovations they should be implemented in conjunction with TDM incentives that encourage transit use and Smart Growth development policies that create compact, walkable neighborhoods around transit stations.[109]

Evidence from North American cities indicates that public transit improvements can significantly increase transit ridership and reduce automobile travel. For example, transit ridership increased in Seattle, Pittsburgh, Houston, Austin, San Antonio, Detroit, and Las Vegas after they increased or restructured service to increase passenger convenience and efficiency,[110] and even larger gains are possible with comprehensive programs that integrate service expansions with technological innovations such as improved user information and more convenient fare payment systems.[111] The Bus Rapid Transit Standard defines various service design features that can increase efficiency, convenience, integration, and ridership; this can guide bus transit improvements.[112] Residents of transit-oriented neighborhoods tend to own about half as many vehicles and generate about half as many vehicle trips as in automobile-oriented areas.[113]

During and after pandemics, extra effort will be required to ensure that public transit minimizes contagion risks. This can include improved cleaning and ventilation, reduced crowding, and providing accurate and timely information to passengers.[114] Such policies can minimize public transit contagion risks, which increases user confidence and ridership.[115]

Mobility as a Service (MaaS)

By integrating various travel modes and services MaaS can support other New Mobilities and increase their use.[116] It can include discounts and incentives for users to choose the most efficient option for each trip. It can directly benefit users and, by shifting travel to resource-efficient modes, provide community benefits. Mobility apps in Helsinki, Finland; Gothenburg, Sweden; De Lijn, Belgium; Hamburg and Karlsruhe, Germany; Madrid, Spain; Singapore; and the entire country of Denmark allow users to easily find, reserve, and pay for bus, tram, metro, taxis, bike- and carsharing, plus public parking.[117]

Communities and service providers should support MaaS development as part of multimodal transportation planning and TDM programs.[118] To be successful, MaaS requires professional organizations and governments to establish data sharing and payment system standards. Public transit, vehicle sharing, ridehailing, and conventional taxi organizations should be encouraged or required to develop integrated apps and payment systems. These services should be planned and regulated to achieve community goals, including universal design (for example, by indicating which services accommodate mobility aides and other special needs), affordability, congestion reductions, safety, and emission reductions.[119] Governments can use MaaS for their own activities—for example, by providing employees and clients with mobility subsidies that can be used for any mode, instead of only offering free parking.

Telework

Telework, including telecommuting, e-commerce, e-medicine, and e-government, can provide many benefits, including consumer savings, vehicle travel reductions, and improved access for people who cannot or should not drive. Because it virtually eliminates contagion risk, telework has proven to be particularly useful during the current pandemic. Employers, businesses, and governments should develop telework policies and programs and provide appropriate support.

However, telework is unsuitable for many activities, jobs, and people, including many disadvantaged people who lack suitable equipment and workspaces.[120] As a result, telework should generally be optional rather than mandatory, and public policies should provide appropriate support, such as training and high-speed internet services when needed to help residents use telecommunications. Governments should review and update regulations related to working conditions and home-based employment to allow home offices and protect worker rights. Because it encourages dispersed development, it should be implemented in conjunction with anti-sprawl policies.

Governments and telecommunications organizations should set telecommunications service standards that are adequate for telework and establish targets for providing that level of service to all households. Some governments are partnering with service providers to provide more affordable and efficient high-speed internet services. For example, Chattanooga, Tennessee, developed its municipal fiber networks to support its growing tech sectors and help residents access public services including e-medicine.[121] Federal and state grants through the Department of Transportation and agencies can help expand local fiber networks as part of smart city initiatives.

Tunnel Roads and Pneumatic Tube Transport

Tunnel roads and pneumatic tube transport are in the developmental stage, so their costs benefits, and commercial feasibility are uncertain. Governments and professional organizations can help define the performance, safety, and environmental standards they must meet in order to operate in various conditions. These facilities and services should be evaluated, planned, and regulated to ensure consistency with strategic community goals. For example, to achieve congestion and emission reduction goals, tunnel roads should be planned and managed to favor shared and electric vehicles, and regulated and priced to prevent them from increasing total vehicle traffic, particularly in congested areas.

If these services meet performance and safety standards, are cost efficient, and can attract sufficient investment, public policies may support their implementation. If pneumatic tube transport proves to be safe and efficient, public policies may encourage it as a substitute for air travel.

Aviation Innovation

Delivery drones, air taxis, and supersonic jets tend to be faster but more expensive and impose greater external costs than alternatives such as conventional courier deliveries, automobiles, public transport, and subsonic aviation. While these modes may be justified for special, high-value uses, such as emergency deliveries to isolated areas, there appears to be little justification for large-scale commercial uses such as delivery of common goods, commuting, or tourism.[122]

The World Economic Forum developed the following Urban Sky Principles to guide air taxi planning.[123]

1. *Safety:* New aviation modes should be as safe as current air travel.
2. *Sustainability:* New aviation modes must improve environmental outcomes.
3. *Equity of access:* New air transport must improve mobility for disadvantaged communities.

4. *Low noise:* Noise disturbance should be minimized by vehicle design, facility siting, and route planning.
5. *Multimodal connectivity:* New aviation modes should seamlessly connect with other modes.
6. *Local workforce development:* New aviation modes should create employment opportunities for local residents.
7. *Purpose-driven data sharing:* New aviation services should share data with all stakeholders to allow informed planning and management decisions.

Governments and professional organizations should define the specific performance and safety standards that these services must meet in order to operate in a community. They should also establish regulations to minimize external costs, as well as fees to compensate for their negative impacts and encourage efficiency.[124] For example, a government could establish drone and air taxi operating rules and noise standards, air space user fees that compensate for the risk, noise, and intrusion they impose on communities, plus tracking and enforcement programs. Similarly, supersonic jets should pay additional fuel taxes to compensate for their high noise and climate emissions.

Mobility Prioritization

Mobility prioritization uses information, pricing, and incentives to favor higher-value trips and more efficient modes. This increases overall transportation system efficiency, which helps reduce traffic problems and infrastructure costs. Mobility prioritization is a form of transportation demand management.

The following policies and services support mobility prioritization:[125]

*   Real-time traffic information systems that encourage travelers to avoid congested conditions.
*   Road and curb space management that favors higher-value trips (such as freight vehicles) and space-efficient modes (such as carpools, microtransit and buses).
*   Efficient road and parking pricing, with higher prices under congested conditions.
*   Commute trip reduction and mobility management marketing programs that encourage travelers to use resource-efficient modes.

Mobility prioritization supports and is supported by other New Mobilities, including active and public transport improvements, microtransit, and logistics management. By favoring space-efficient modes, mobility prioritization gives travelers more incentives to use active and micro modes, shared vehicles, and public transit services, which can create a positive cycle of increased demand and improved services. By favoring higher-value trips, it supports logistics management.

Many US cities have high-occupancy vehicle lanes and some have time-variable road tolls that have higher rates during peak periods and lower rates off-peak.[126] Several cities around the world, including London, Oslo, Singapore, and Stockholm, have implemented successful area-wide decongestion tolls.[127]

Logistics Management

Logistics management can provide many community benefits including efficient shipping and courier services that support local economic development, plus benefits from reduced truck traffic.[128] Regional and local governments should develop freight transportation plans to guide logistics management implementation. This process should include freight infrastructure planning, TDM incentives and mobility priority to favor freight vehicle over lower value traffic, and development of urban consolidation centers (UCCs) to provide efficient local distribution.[129] These should anticipate and incorporate innovative technologies and services such as automated dispatching and freight vehicle navigation systems, electric and autonomous delivery vehicles, and cargo bikes.[130]

For example, about eighty German cities have set up "City Logistics" projects whereby shipments are consolidated outside the city limits and better organized within the city.[131] The municipality, chambers of commerce, and large haulers set up a trans-shipment facility and a new company that provides coordinated delivery services within the city. These services use vehicles with state-of-the-art air and noise emission reduction features. The report *Making Urban Freight Logistics More Sustainable* recommends the following local policies for more efficient logistics management:[132]

- Integrate logistics into transportation and land use planning.
- Develop a City Logistics plan and manager.
- Encourage shifts to resource-efficient freight modes.
- Regulate freight vehicle access times.

- Regulate curbs and parking to favor freight delivery.
- Require and encourage low-polluting freight vehicles.
- Regulate freight vehicle routes, speed, and loads.
- Apply efficient road and parking pricing.
- Plan on- and off-street loading zones.
- Develop urban consolidation centers and integrated freight programs.
- Develop real-time freight vehicle information and traffic control.
- Encourage eco-driving (more fuel-efficient driving habits).
- Impose anti-idling regulations.
- Develop green freight recognition and certification programs.

Chapter 8

Conclusion

I hope that you've enjoyed this ramble through the past, present, and potential futures of transportation innovations. Let's review our journey highlights.

Lessons from the Past

To prepare for the future, it is important to understand the past. Chapter 2 examines how previous transportation innovations affected people and communities. During the last 120 years, new transportation technologies increased our mobility by an order of magnitude but increased economic, social, and environmental costs by similar amounts. During this period, planning favored faster more expensive modes over slower more affordable and resource-efficient modes. Governments made huge investments in highways and forced property owners to subsidize an abundant supply of parking. Active modes (walking, bicycling, and their variants) and public transit received little support. This created automobile-dependent communities where driving is convenient but other modes are often inefficient, difficult, and dangerous to use.

If you are a typical North American adult you own a personal vehicle that you drive about ten thousand annual miles. To do so, you must devote about a fifth of your household budget, and therefore a fifth of your workday, to paying vehicle and residential parking expenses. These cost burdens are an order of magnitude higher than in 1900, and 50 percent more in the United States and Canada than in most other affluent countries. You devote about an hour a day to driving, and more if you have dependents who require frequent chauffeuring. In addition, all this driving imposes significant congestion delays, crash risk, and health costs. If for any reason you cannot, should not, or prefer not to drive, your travel options range from poor to terrible in most areas.

This is not optimal. Many people want more affordable, inclusive, and efficient mobility options. In response, many communities are starting to apply a new planning paradigm that considers a wider range of goals and perspectives, and so supports more multimodal planning, transportation demand management (TDM), and Smart Growth development policies. This has important implications for New Mobility planning. Some of these transportation innovations increase mobility—that is, they increase travel speeds and therefore the distances that we can travel within our limited travel time budgets—and so rate well under the old paradigm, while others are slower but are more affordable, healthy, and resource efficient, and so tend to rate well under the new paradigm. Table 8-1 shows these categories.

Transportation policy debates often reflect these different perspectives. Some people still assume that our primary goal is to increase mobility, and so tend to be frustrated by planning decisions that reflect other priorities and perspectives. However, current demographic and economic

Table 8-1 **Paradigm Perspectives.** Some New Mobilities increase vehicle travel speeds and so rate well under the old planning paradigm. Others are slower but more affordable, resource efficient, and healthy, and so rate well under the new paradigm. Some are contingent, depending on how they are implemented.

Old (Increases Mobility)	Contingent (Depends)	New (Increases Accessibility)
Tunnel Roads		Active and Micromobilities
Pneumatic Tube Transport		Vehicle Sharing and Microtransit
Autonomous Vehicles		Public Transit Innovations
Delivery Drones	Electric Vehicles	Mobility as a Service
Air Taxis	Ridehailing	Mobility Prioritization
Supersonic Jets	Telework	Logistics Management

trends support the new planning paradigm. Although few people want to forgo driving altogether, surveys indicate that, compared with their current travel patterns, many would prefer to drive less, spend less money on transportation, and rely more on non-auto modes, provided those alternatives are convenient, comfortable, and affordable. Similarly, many communities have goals to increase affordability, social equity, public fitness and health, and environmental quality. The new paradigm responds to those emerging consumer preferences and community values.

Planning Principles

For individual users, New Mobility planning is relatively easy: you simply decide whether a new transportation technology or service is worth the cost. People bike, scooter, carshare, and use public transit when these modes offer cost-effective mobility. Similarly, travelers sometimes pay extra for electric vehicles and, in the future, for autonomous vehicles, tunnel roads, air taxis, and supersonic jet travel because they consider the additional benefits worth the extra expense.

However, community planning decisions are more complicated because they often involve trade-offs between numerous goals and interests. Money and road space dedicated to one mode cannot be used for others, and some modes impose significant congestion delay, crash risks, and pollution exposure on others. Planning decisions must balance these conflicting demands.

Fortunately there is practical guidance to help with these decisions. Chapter 3 describes principles for efficient and equitable transportation planning. This means that a planning process should consider all significant goals and perspectives; recognize diverse travel demands; and invest in the most cost-effective transportation improvement options, considering all impacts and goals. Efficiency and equity also require that, as much as possible, users "get what they pay for and pay for what they get," unless subsidies are specifically justified for equity's sake or to achieve strategic goals. These principles can help guide our analysis.

Evaluating the New Mobilities

Chapter 5 uses a comprehensive framework to evaluate the New Mobilities from various perspectives.

How do New Mobilities affect the user experience? Under favorable conditions, active modes, micromobilities, and public transit can be convenient and comfortable, but under unfavorable conditions, they are difficult and unpleasant to use, so improving their facilities and services can provide large direct user benefits and increase their use. Telework, in which telecommunications substitute for physical travel, can also increase users' comfort and convenience but may be difficult and stressful for people who lack suitable equipment, skills, or work space. Although proponents often portray autonomous taxis, tunnel roads, pneumatic tube transport, and supersonic jets as comfortable and enjoyable to use, in practice they will generally be more crowded, noisy, and dirty (particularly autonomous taxis) than alternatives. This may limit their use and commercial viability.

User costs also vary significantly. Active transportation, micro modes, public transit, and telework are generally affordable, even to low-income users. Shared vehicles and ridehailing have relatively high costs per mile of travel but are affordable if used occasionally in conjunction with lower-cost modes. Electric and autonomous vehicles have high ownership costs but low operating costs, in part because electric vehicles do not pay road user taxes. Tunnel roads, pneumatic tube transport, air taxis, and supersonic jets are likely to be expensive and unaffordable to most travelers.

New Mobilities can affect travel time costs in various ways. Some, such as active and public transport improvements, can increase these modes' travel speeds or reduce delays. For example, active mode improvements often include pedestrian and bicycle shortcuts, and public transit improvements and mobility prioritization can include special lanes or pricing that reduces delays for higher-value trips and more efficient modes. Some New Mobilities, including public transit and autonomous vehicles, allow passengers to rest or work while traveling, which reduces their travel time unit costs. Air taxis and supersonic jets can increase travel speeds for a portion of a journey, but their door-to-door time savings are often modest considering the time required to access terminals and board aircraft.

New Mobilities vary in their travel impacts—that is, how and how much people travel. Active modes, micromobilities, public transit improvements, Mobility as a Service (MaaS), and logistics management often attract travelers who would otherwise drive, reducing total vehicle travel. Ridesharing, electric and autonomous vehicles, and tunnel roads are likely to increase total vehicle travel unless implemented with strong TDM incentives such as decongestion pricing (road tolls that are higher under congested conditions). Telework reduces some vehicle trips but tends to increase others and encourages sprawled development, which tends to increase total vehicle travel unless implemented with TDM incentives and Smart Growth policies.

Mobility prioritization is a unique category of New Mobilities. It is not a mode; rather, it applies new technologies and management practices to favor higher-value trips and more efficient modes over lower-value and less-efficient alternatives. It can include improved navigation and payment apps that can offer targeted discounts, rewards, and games that encourage travelers to choose the most resource-efficient option for each trip.

New Mobilities vary significantly in their external costs, including infrastructure subsidies (such as road and parking facility costs funded by general taxes or incorporated into rents and the prices of other goods), traffic congestion, barrier effect (delay to pedestrians and bicyclists), crash risk, noise, and pollution emissions imposed on other people. Active travel, micro modes, public transit, and microtransit generally impose much lower external costs than automobile travel measured per passenger-mile, and because they are slower users tend to travel fewer miles per year, so people who rely on these modes tend to impose much lower total external costs, measured per person-year. Mobility as a Service, mobility prioritization, and logistics management tend to reduce external costs indirectly by encouraging travelers to choose resource-efficient modes. Ridehailing, electric and autonomous vehicles, tunnel roads, and air taxis tend to increase total vehicle travel and therefore external costs, unless implemented with TDM incentives and anti-sprawl policies.

New Mobilities vary significantly in the degree they support or contradict various community goals, including affordability, infrastructure savings, social equity, public health, contagion avoidance, resource conservation, and strategic objectives to create more compact, multimodal communities. Modes that are affordable, resource efficient, and healthy to use, and encourage more compact urban development, tend to achieve the greatest range of goals, while those that are expensive, are resource intensive, and encourage sprawl tend to contradict these goals.

Chapter 6 systematically evaluates the New Mobilities according to eight community planning goals using a seven-point scale. Figure 8-1 compares their overall ratings.

The highest-rated modes are active and micromobilities and public transport improvements because they help achieve virtually all planning goals. Vehicle sharing, Mobility as a Service, mobility prioritization, and logistics management also provide numerous benefits but are less effective at achieving affordability, health, and contagion avoidance. Ridehailing,

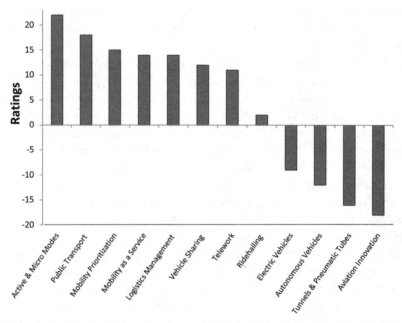

Figure 8-1 New Mobilities' Ratings According to Eight Planning Goals. This figure compares New Mobilities' overall ratings according to eight community goals. The methodology used to calculate these ratings is described in Chapter 6. (Based on Table 6-11.)

microtransit, and telework have positive ratings but with current policies are likely to increase total vehicle travel and sprawl, increasing some costs. As a result, their benefits are much larger if they are implemented with TDM incentives and anti-sprawl policies.

Electric and autonomous vehicles, tunnel roads, pneumatic tube transport, and aviation innovations have negative overall ratings because they provide a limited variety of benefits, are expensive, and tend to increase total vehicle travel and therefore external costs. This indicates that they should be implemented with strong TDM policies to ensure that they are used only when their benefits exceed their costs.

New Mobilities tend to be most efficient and beneficial if implemented as part of an integrated package that includes various new modes and services, plus TDM incentives to maximize their benefits. An integrated set of New Mobilities can create a truly multimodal transportation system that allows households to own fewer vehicles, drive less, use more resource-efficient modes, save money, and be better off overall as a result.

You may disagree with some of these ratings or believe that some goals deserve more weight than others, and impacts may vary significantly depending on specific circumstances and implementation practices. For example, ridehailing and electric and autonomous vehicles rate higher in suburban and rural locations but lower in dense urban conditions. However, the basic results are robust: modes that are affordable and resource efficient tend to provide the most diverse benefits and the least external costs, and so help achieve the greatest range of community goals.

From Optimistic to Realistic Analysis

Because New Mobilities are currently under development, it is difficult to predict their ultimate impacts. Some industry advocates make optimistic claims about their benefits. For example, some people predict that by 2030 shared, electric, and autonomous vehicles will be so cheap, efficient, and comfortable that travelers will choose them for 95 percent of trips, and they will virtually eliminate traffic congestion, traffic crashes, and pollution problems. These claims are based on experience with other electronic technologies such as digital cameras, smartphones, and personal computers, which transformed those industries and our lives. However, those predictions are probably exaggerated.

Motor vehicles involve much greater risks, last much longer, and cost far more than most consumer electronic devices. A camera, phone, or computer failure can be frustrating, but a vehicle control failure can be frustrating *and* dangerous. In addition, motor vehicles require costly public infrastructure. As a result, autonomous vehicles require far more regulation, testing, and public planning than personal electronics. Optimistically, Level 4 autonomous vehicles, which can operate without driver intervention in certain conditions, will be commercially available in some jurisdictions by the mid-2020s, but most experts conclude that Level 5 vehicles, which can operate autonomously under all normal conditions, will take much longer to become commercially available and decades more before they dominate the vehicle fleet.

Optimists predict that autonomous taxi fares will average just twenty cents per vehicle-mile, and microtransit fares just ten cents per passenger-mile, but these estimates ignore many costs required for such services including cleaning and repairs, safety and security support, road user fees, empty vehicle-miles, administration, and profits. For example, autonomous taxis will probably need to visit a cleaning station every five to fifteen trips, which will add expenses and vehicle-miles. For security's sake they will require monitoring—people in control rooms watching for dangerous conditions and irresponsible behavior—which will also be costly. For efficiency and fairness, they should be charged road user fees ranging from five cents per vehicle-mile on minor roads to more than twenty cents per vehicle mile for driving on congested urban roadways. Demand-response microtransit also requires additional vehicle-miles and time to pick up and deliver passengers. Considering these factors, autonomous taxi services will probably cost fifty to eighty cents per vehicle-mile, which is cheaper than a human-operated taxi but more expensive than private automobile travel. Similarly, microtransit services will probably cost twenty-five to forty cents per passenger-mile, which is cheaper than providing conventional transit services in areas with low ridership but more expensive than conventional transit operating on busy corridors. As a result, microtransit may be appropriate for some locations and times, but it will not substitute for high-capacity rail and bus transit.

Optimists also tend to exaggerate these vehicles' ability to reduce traffic congestion, crash risk, and pollution emissions. Under certain conditions, particularly if they are given dedicated highway lanes, autonomous vehicles can significantly increase traffic flow, but this benefit will be offset if they increase total vehicle travel or are programmed to maximize passenger comfort and safety rather than traffic speed. Although they can reduce driver errors, autonomous vehicles will introduce new risks including hardware and software failures, malicious hacking, and increased risk taking by other road users. Electric vehicles reduce climate emissions by 50 to 75 percent, depending on how electricity is generated, but because of their heavy batteries, they increase harmful rubber particulates produced by tire wear. As a result, these new technologies do not eliminate external costs or the justification for vehicle travel reduction targets.

Similarly, advocates claim that electric air taxis are a sustainable mode since they will be quieter and less polluting than helicopters, but total noise and pollution are likely to increase if city skies are filled with thousands of these aircraft, as the industry hopes.

Can New Mobilities Increase Affordability?

New Mobilities vary significantly in their costs and therefore their ability to provide consumer savings and affordability. Let's see how various options affect user costs.

Currently, a typical motorist drives about ten thousand annual miles and spends about $5,000 in annual vehicle expenses, plus $1,000 for residential parking, and occasionally uses shared vehicles (ridehailing and rental cars), shared trips (public transit travel), and active travel (walking and bicycling). Together, these total about $6,500 per year. Assuming that affordability requires that households spend no more than 10 percent of their income on transportation,[1] this is only affordable for a one-vehicle household that earns at least $65,000 annual income, or a two-vehicle household that earns at least $130,000 per year.

Autonomous electric vehicles will cost significantly more for additional hardware and software, periodic battery replacements, additional servicing requirements, subscriptions to advanced mapping services, plus parking spaces wired for battery charging systems. Because of their greater convenience, typical autonomous vehicle owners are expected to drive 25 percent more annual miles than they would with a human-operated vehicle. As a result, their total transportation expenses are estimated to increase to $8,960 per year. This is affordable for a single-vehicle household that earns at least $89,600 annual income, or a two-vehicle household that earns at least $179,200 per year.

However, with New Mobilities they could give up vehicle ownership and rely on multiple modes, traveling four thousand annual miles by shared vehicles (autonomous taxi), four thousand miles by shared trips (public transit and autonomous microtransit), and one thousand miles by active and micro modes (walking, bicycling, e-scooter, and e-bike), resulting in $3,700 total annual transportation expenditures, which is affordable for a single-adult household that earns a $37,000 per year, or a two-adult household that earns $74,000 annually. By living in a compact, multimodal neighborhood they could further reduce their motor vehicle travel, traveling two thousand annual miles by shared vehicles, two thousand miles by shared trips, and two thousand miles by active and micro modes, resulting in just $2,000 annual transportation expenditures, which is affordable for a single-adult household that earns $20,000 per year, or a two-adult household that earns $40,000 annually.

Figure 8-2 compares these options. This makes an important point. A high-annual-mileage lifestyle is expensive with both current and future technologies. It may be affordable for higher-income households but tends to impose significant financial strains on those with below-average incomes, particularly because automobiles occasionally have large unexpected expenses due to mechanical failures, crashes, or traffic violations. Multimodal transportation, which uses a combination of shared vehicles

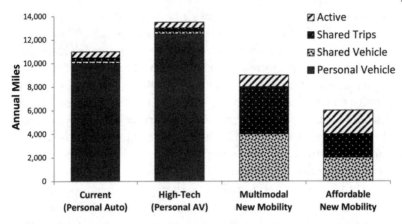

Figure 8-2 New Mobilities' Impacts on Travel and Transportation Expenses. Currently, a typical adult owns a personal automobile that is driven ten thousand annual miles and only occasionally uses shared vehicles (ridehailing and car rentals), shared trips (public transit), or active modes (walking and bicycling). With High-Tech New Mobility, they own a personal autonomous vehicle (AV), which increases their annual mileage and total expenses. With Multimodal New Mobility, they can forgo vehicle ownership and rely on a combination of shared vehicles, shared trips, and active travel. Affordable New Mobility relies equally on shared vehicle, shared trip, and active travel. This is only feasible for households located in compact, multimodal neighborhoods. Dollar values indicate total annual transportation costs. (Assumes that private and shared vehicles cost, on average, $0.50 per mile, ridehailing costs $1.80 per mile, shared trips $0.30 per mile, active travel $0.10 per mile, current personal vehicles require a residential parking space that costs $1,000 per year, and electric autonomous vehicles require a residential parking space with a Level 2 recharging station that costs $1,200 per year.)

and trips, plus active travel, can provide significant savings, but the only transportation system that is truly affordable to most low-income households results from living in a compact, multimodal neighborhood where travel distances are shorter and most common services and activities are easily accessed by active and public transport.

Of course, these impacts vary depending on conditions. For example, because they are space efficient and minimize pollution emissions, active and public transport, vehicle sharing, MaaS, mobility prioritization, and logistics management are most efficient and beneficial in denser urban areas where congestion and pollution problems are most severe. On the other hand, ridehailing, electric, and autonomous vehicles provide more convenient, door-to-door travel but are space intensive and so are more appropriate in suburban and rural areas. All of these modes become more cost effective and beneficial if implemented with TDM incentives that encourage travelers to choose the most efficient option for each trip—so, for example, automobile owners are encouraged to walk, bike, rideshare, and use public transit when possible, and autonomous vehicle users are dissuaded from programming their cars to drive in circles in order to avoid paying parking fees. These impacts also depend on future technological progress. If autonomous vehicles, delivery drones, air taxis, and supersonic jets become as safe, quiet, affordable, and efficient as optimists predict, their net benefits may rise, but decision-makers should be skeptical and demand objective evidence.

No single mode can serve all travel demands; travelers, particularly those with low incomes, need an integrated set of low- and moderate-priced modes. This indicates that, to maximize affordability, planning should favor lower-cost New Mobilities, including improvements to active and micromobilities, public transit and microtransit, MaaS, and telework, with special attention to creating convenient connections among them. It also requires Smart Growth development policies to ensure that any household, particularly those with lower incomes, can find appropriate housing in compact, multimodal neighborhoods. Together, these can create truly affordable and efficient transportation systems where travelers can choose the combination of mobility options that best meets their needs.

Envisioning an Optimal Future Transportation System

What would happen if these recommendations are implemented? The following section describes the results. New Mobilities are in bold.

To be efficient and equitable, an optimal transportation system must be diverse and encourage resource-efficient, affordable, and healthy modes. It therefore has excellent **active transportation**, **micromobilities**, and **public transit** services. Where demand exists, it provides **scooter-**, **bike-**, **e-bike-**, and **carsharing** services. Planning is comprehensive and multimodal. Transportation agencies consider all modes and impacts and can invest at least as much money and road space to accommodate a bicycle, scooter, or public transit trip as would be spent to accommodate an automobile trip, and more if that helps achieve strategic planning goals. Roadway planning applies *complete streets* principles, which ensure that roads accommodate diverse users and uses.[2] Transportation facilities and services reflect *universal design* standards, which ensure that they accommodate people with disabilities and other special needs.[3]

An optimal transportation system emphasizes accessibility. Residential neighborhoods are planned to ensure that commonly used services, such as shops, restaurants, parks, and schools, are located within convenient walking distance of most homes. Development policies ensure that households with low incomes can find suitable housing in a walkable neighborhood where it is easy to get around without a car. Streets are designed for comfort, with landscaping for beauty and shade and street furniture such as benches and shelters. Local parks and public buildings are located and designed to encourage positive interactions among neighbors. Parking minimums are eliminated and parking is unbundled (rented separately from building space) so residents are no longer forced to pay for costly parking spaces they don't need. Parking facilities are efficiently managed to minimize the number of spaces needed.

An optimal transportation system favors resource-efficient modes. Streets have sidewalks, crosswalks, and traffic calming, so they are safe and comfortable for **active** and **micro modes**, and often include shortcuts for these modes. High-quality **public transit** and **microtransit** provide frequent, fast, comfortable, and affordable connections between neighborhoods. Large cities have **Urban Rail Networks** with attractive stations, and most cities have **bus rapid transit (BRT)** systems with functional and comfortable stops. Major roadways have HOV lanes and bus priority features to ensure that bus travel is fast and efficient. Transit systems use **information and pricing technologies** to provide real-time vehicle arrival and crowding information, automated touchless payment systems, and passenger security enhancements. Transit vehicles have free **Wi-Fi services** and other passenger amenities. **Mobility marketing** promotes public transit as an efficient, safe, and enjoyable way to travel.

Bus stops and train stations are designed for passenger convenience and comfort. They often include coffee shops and convenience stores and are sometimes integrated into civic or commercial buildings. Stations are multimodal **mobility hubs** that support **Mobility as a Service**, including **ridehailing, carsharing, scooter-** and **bikesharing**, and **efficient parking**, with navigation and payment apps for seamless connections.

An optimal transportation system uses **mobility prioritization** to favor higher-value travel, such as emergency and freight vehicles, and more space-efficient modes such as **public transit** and **rideshare** vehicles. Urban regions have comprehensive **logistical management** to help businesses coordinate shipping and distribution. Transportation is **efficiently priced**, so motorists pay directly for using roads and parking facilities, with higher rates under congested conditions. Fossil fuel prices increase steadily to encourage shifts to alternative fuels and more resource-efficient modes.

Larger employers have **commute trip reduction programs** that encourage employees to use efficient travel options, including **telework**. Major activity centers have transportation management associations that provide transportation and parking management services. Mobility management marketing programs encourage travelers to use efficient travel options, with targeted campaigns that highlight affordability, health, and community benefits to appropriate groups.

An optimal transportation system encourages travelers to choose the most appropriate vehicle for each trip. It favors **vehicle sharing** over private vehicle travel. Convenient and affordable **bike-, scooter-,** and **car-sharing; taxi and ridehailing**; and **delivery** services are widely available. Most vehicles are **electric**, particularly high-annual-mileage vehicles such as freight vehicles, buses, and taxis.

An optimal transportation system encourages innovation. It establishes performance standards and testing protocols for new transportation technologies and services, including **autonomous vehicles, tunnel roads, pneumatic tube transport, delivery drones**, and **air taxis**. High-mileage and high-impact users, such as buses, freight trucks, taxis, and ridehailing vehicles, are encouraged to quickly adopt **electric vehicle** technologies.

You might find these conclusions disappointing. Some people envision a high-technology, high-mobility future filled with autonomous vehicles, tunnel roads, pneumatic tube transport, delivery drones, air taxis, and supersonic jets. Those modes seem exciting and glamorous. However, I suspect that proponents overlook some important details. Those high-speed modes tend to be expensive and uncomfortable. For example, autonomous taxis may be cheaper than human-operated taxis but more expensive than other local travel modes, and so will only be affordable as a minor part of a multimodal transportation menu that also includes plenty of walking, bicycling, and public transit travel. Autonomous taxis will lack the services provided by a human driver: luggage handling, advice on local attractions, and ensuring that passengers arrive safely at their front door. Passengers will sometimes encounter garbage, odors, and suspicious stains left by previous occupants. As a result, rather than being exciting and glamorous, autonomous taxis will probably be an inferior option; many travelers will willingly pay extra for the full-service human-operated taxis.

Similarly, tunnel roads, pneumatic tube transport, and air taxis are likely to be more costly and less comfortable than alternatives for most trips. For example, air taxis may be cheaper and quieter than helicopters but more costly, nosier, and less comfortable than normal car travel. Although these modes can significantly increase speeds during some portions of a journey, their door-to-door time savings are generally modest. For example, supersonic jet travel may cut in half the in-air time required for some intercontinental trips, but this typically only represents a 30 percent reduction in door-to-door journey times, and because of its very high fares, supersonic jet travel will be cost effective only for people who value their travel time at thousands of dollars per hour.

Although active and public transport are considered less exciting and glamorous, improving these modes can significantly increase users' speed, convenience, comfort, health, and enjoyment. For example, short-cut paths can significantly reduce the time required to walk or bicycle to destinations, and a combination of automated boarding, bus lanes, and mobility prioritization can significantly increase public transit travel speeds and comfort. By attracting travelers who would otherwise drive, these improvements can reduce external costs. As a result, these less glamorous modes generally provide the greatest returns on investments.

This is not to suggest that high-speed, high-cost modes, such as autonomous vehicles, tunnel roads, pneumatic tube transport, delivery drones, air taxis, and supersonic jets, should be forbidden; they may be very appropriate for some applications. However, because of their limited benefits and high external costs, there is no reason that public policies should encourage their use.

Our Challenge

The analysis in this book indicates that it is possible to incorporate New Mobilities into our transportation system in ways that achieve community goals. Our policies and planning practices can favor more efficient and inclusive modes, use TDM incentives to encourage travelers to choose the best mobility option for each trip, and apply Smart Growth policies to create more accessible, multimodal communities. This can create a far more affordable, efficient, and healthy transportation system than what currently exists in most North American communities. Our biggest problem would be to determine how best to spend our thousands of dollars in annual savings, how to reuse all of the road space and land currently devoted to motor vehicle traffic and parking facilities, and how to spend all of the additional time we've saved when we drive less and rely more on local services. Such sweet problems!

However, this transformation faces huge challenges. Most North Americans are accustomed to an automobile-dependent, highly mobile lifestyle and have little experience with an efficient, multimodal transportation system. People work hard to afford a nice automobile, which they rely on for most of their travel needs. These vehicles provide status, convenience, privacy, and security, while other modes are considered inferior. Policies to encourage efficient travel are called transportation demand management, which is abbreviated *TDM* and pronounced *tedium*, which sounds terrible.

Our challenge, therefore, is political. To be successful we need to frame these issues in a positive way so citizens will support vehicle travel reduction targets, multimodal planning, TDM incentives, and Smart Growth development policies. Fortunately, we have a terrific product: a more efficient and multimodal transportation system can provide large financial savings, health benefits, community benefits, and fun. We need to help people envision this better future and support policy changes that help achieve this long-term vision.

The New Mobilities tend to increase the potential and the urgency of these reforms. For example, during the COVID-19 pandemic many people became accustomed to telework, scooters and bicycles became more popular, and many communities created new pedestrian and bicycling facilities. Some of these changes will probably continue into the future. On the other hand, the traffic problems caused by ridehailing and curbside deliveries are increasing in many cities, harbingers of the more severe problems that are likely to result as more households purchase electric and autonomous vehicles.

Our job is to frighten, reassure, and plan. We need to scare decision-makers and the general public about the potential problems that are likely to result from unregulated New Mobilities. We also need to reassure them that excellent solutions are available. We must help create a positive vision of a better future and identify the specific policies and programs that can achieve it.

Impacts on Freedom—A Bonus Perspective

Let's explore another way to evaluate New Mobilities: impacts on people's freedom.

Private automobile travel is often promoted as a source of personal freedom. This implies that policies to encourage other modes threaten people's freedom. TDM incentives are sometimes criticized as a "war on cars," and Smart Growth development policies are criticized as a "war on suburbs." Let's examine those claims.

In fact, conventional planning tends to reduce people's freedom in several ways. Policies that create automobile dependency and sprawl assume that everybody wants a conventional, high-consumption lifestyle, with an expensive automobile and a large suburban house. These policies

Table 8-2 New Mobilities' Impacts on Freedoms. New Mobilities can impact freedoms in many ways. Multimodal transportation tends to maximize the greatest variety of freedoms for the greatest number of people. Some New Mobilities have mixed impacts on motorists because they reduce road space for cars but also reduce overall congestion and drivers' chauffeuring burdens.

	Mobility for Drivers	Mobility for Non-Drivers	Financial	From Danger	From Guilt
Active Travel and Micromobilities	Mixed	Large increase	Increase	Increase	Increase
Vehicle Sharing	Increase	Increase	Increase	Increase	Increase
Ridehailing and Microtransit	Mixed	Increase	Increase	Increase	Mixed
Electric Vehicles	Increase	No impact	Mixed	No impact	Increase
Autonomous Vehicles	Increase	No impact	Reduction	Increase	Mixed
Public Transport Innovations	Mixed	Large increase	Increase	Increase	Increase
Mobility as a Service	Mixed	Increase	Increase	Increase	Increase
Telework	Increase	Increase	Increase	Increase	Increase
Tunnel Roads and Pneumatic Tube Transport	Increase	Increase	Mixed	Mixed	Reduction
Aviation Innovation	No Impact	Increase	Reduction	Reduction	Reduction
Mobility Prioritization	Mixed	Increase	Mixed	Increase	Increase
Logistics Management	Increase	Increase	Increase	Increase	Increase

force people to drive more annual miles, consume more resources, spend more money, work longer hours, and impose much larger external costs than optimal for their happiness or our planet. This may be suitable for some people, but for others it is a bad fit. These policies are particularly harmful to physically and economically disadvantaged groups, who receive smaller benefits but bear large costs from automobile travel. As a result, automobile dependency is inherently unfair.

Table 8-2 examines how New Mobilities affect five types of freedom: mobility for drivers, independent mobility for non-drivers (and therefore motorists' chauffeuring burdens), financial freedom, freedom from danger, and freedom from guilt caused by the external costs that travel activities impose on other people.

Planning for Resilience

This book was written during the 2020 COVID-19 outbreak. This experience highlights the importance of planning for resilience and provides information that can be used to minimize contagion risks.[4]

Resilience refers to a community's ability to respond to economic, social, and environmental shocks. Resilience planning requires effective emergency management programs and robust design standards for essential infrastructure, plus diverse and redundant transportation systems that can respond to unexpected demands and conditions.

To respond to pandemics, transportation systems must minimize contagion risks, provide adequate access and physical activity during quarantines and travel restrictions, and address the mobility needs of frontline workers and people who lose incomes.[5]

Because they are unenclosed, active and micro modes tend to have minimal contagion risk, as does telework. If they follow hygiene protocols, carsharing and public transit have moderate contagion risk, while ridehailing, pneumatic tube transport, air taxis, and supersonic jets have higher risks because they require multiple passengers to travel in enclosed vehicles for extended periods of time. Although driving alone incurs minimal contagion risk, most motorists carry passengers, at least occasionally, which explains why automobile-dependent areas tend to have higher infection rates than compact, walkable neighborhoods.[6]

To prepare for future pandemics, communities should improve walking, bicycling, and micromobilities; provide more affordable transportation options; reduce total vehicle travel; and create more affordable housing with amenities such as balconies and high-speed internet access, in walkable neighborhoods.

Implications for Developing Countries

Although much of the information in this book is from North America, most of the conclusions are transferable to other regions. Cities around the world experience severe traffic congestion and parking problems, crash risk, pollution, and inequity. Many developing countries are experiencing rapid growth in vehicle ownership that, if uncontrolled, will exacerbate these problems, making their cities less efficient, equitable, and livable. To avoid these problems, cities must create multimodal transportation systems that include affordable and resource-efficient New Mobilities such as active and micromodes, public transit innovations, telework, and bike-sharing, with strong TDM incentives to limit automobile traffic to what is optimal. As a result, most conclusions and recommendations in this book apply in developing as well as developed countries, although they should be adjusted as appropriate to reflect local conditions.[7]

What Next?

According to ancient Greek mythology, the clever craftsman Daedalus made wings from feathers and wax for himself and his son, Icarus, to escape their exile on the island of Crete. Daedalus warned Icarus not to fly so low that the sea's dampness could clog their feathers, nor so high that the sun's heat could melt them. But flying was too much fun! Icarus ignored his father's instructions; he flew so high that his wings melted and he fell to death. This is a good metaphor for the New Mobilities. They are clever innovations, but they introduce new risks that can lead to disaster. We must accept their practical limits.

Planning is concerned with our future, and therefore our hopes and fears. Technological development expands what we can accomplish, helping to achieve our dreams, but can also have unexpected consequences, and so should invoke a little fear. During the last century new technologies significantly increased our mobility. Has this made us happier, healthier, or wealthier? Has it improved our lives and communities? Are we freer? The overall results are mixed. With wiser planning, we can do better!

The analysis in this book indicates that new transportation technologies and services do not change the basic principles of good planning, including the importance of comprehensive analysis, consumer sovereignty, and cost efficiency. These principles apply equally to new as well as old mobilities.

New Mobilities are no panacea. No magic thinking please! There are good reasons to be skeptical of optimistic claims about emerging transportation technologies and services. New Mobilities can provide significant benefits, but they can also impose significant costs. To maximize their benefits we must be discerning; communities must be willing to say "no" when necessary to ensure that these innovations truly benefit everyone.

Chapter 1

1. Christine Cosgrove and Phyllis Orrick (2004). "The Future That Never Was: Lessons from Visions of Transportation." *TR News 235*. Transportation Research Board, Nov/Dec, pp. 3–9; Joseph Corn (1984). *Yesterday's Tomorrows: Past Vision of the American Future*. Smithsonian Institute, www.museumon mainstreet.org/content/yesterdays-tomorrows.
2. *Weekend Magazine* (1961). "Will Life Be Worth Living in 2,000 AD?" July 22.
3. Irem Kok et al. (2017). *Rethinking Transportation 2020–2030: Disruption of Transportation and the Collapse of the Internal-Combustion Vehicle & Oil Industries*. RethinkX, www.wsdot.wa.gov/publications/fulltext/ProjectDev /PSEProgram/Disruption-of-Transportation.pdf.
4. Jacob Mason, Lew Fulton, and Zane McDonald (2015). *A Global High Shift Cycling Scenario: The Potential for Dramatically Increasing Bicycle and E-bike Use in Cities Around the World*. ITDP and the University of California, https://itdpdotorg.wpengine.com/wp-content/uploads/2015/11/A -Global-High-Shift-Cycling-Scenario_Nov-2015.pdf.
5. Aslak Fyhri and Hanne Beate Sundfør (2020). "Do People Who Buy E-bikes Cycle More?" *Transportation Research Part D 86*, https://doi.org/10.1016/j .trd.2020.102422.

Chapter 2

1. Todd Litman (2020). *Our World Accelerated: How 120 Years of Transportation Progress Affected Our Lives and Communities*. Victoria Transport Policy Institute, www.vtpi.org/TIEI.pdf.
2. Asif Ahmed and Peter Stopher (2014). "Seventy Minutes Plus or Minus 10—A Review of Travel Time Budget Studies." *Transport Reviews 34*(5), pp. 607–625, https://doi.org/10.1080/01441647.2014.946460.
3. Todd Litman (2001). "Generated Traffic: Implications for Transport Planning." *ITE Journal 71*(4), pp. 38–47, www.vtpi.org/gentraf.pdf.
4. Clay McShane (1994). *Down the Asphalt Path*. New York: Columbia University Press, p. 135.

5. Jeffrey Brinkman and Jeffrey Lin (2019). *Freeway Revolts!* Working Paper 19-29. Federal Reserve Bank of Philadelphia, https://doi.org/10.21799/frbp .wp.2019.29.

6. NACTO (2016). *Global Street Design Guide.* National Association of City Transportation Officials and the Global Designing Cities Initiative, https://global designingcities.org/publication/street-users/.

7. Marc Schlossberg, John Rowell, Dave Amos, and Kelly Sanford (2013). *Rethinking Streets: An Evidence-Based Guide to 25 Complete Street Transformations.* University of Oregon's Sustainable Cities Initiative, www.rethinkingstreets .com.

8. ITDP (2012). *The Life and Death of Urban Highways.* Institute for Transportation and Development Policy, www.itdp.org/2012/03/13/the-life-and -death-of-urban-highways/.

9. Giulio Mattioli et al. (2020). "The Political Economy of Car Dependence: A Systems of Provision Approach." *Energy Research & Social Science 66*, https: //doi.org/10.1016/j.erss.2020.101486.

10. Susan Handy (2020). *What California Gains from Reducing Car Dependence.* National Center for Sustainable Transportation, https://escholarship.org/uc /item/0hk0h610.

11. Gregory H. Shill (2019). "Americans Shouldn't Have to Drive, but the Law Insists on It." *The Atlantic,* www.theatlantic.com/ideas/archive/2019/07/car -crashes-arent-always-unavoidable/592447/.

12. SSTI (2018). *Modernizing Mitigation: A Demand-Centered Approach.* State Smart Transportation Initiative and the Mayors Innovation Project, https://ssti .us/2018/09/24/modern-mitigation-a-demand-centered-approach-ssti-sep tember-2018/.

13. ITE (2020). *COVID-19 Resources.* Institute of Transportation Engineers, www .ite.org/about-ite/covid-19-resources/?_zs=MHVdl&_zl=qbii1.

14. Brandon Dupont, Drew Keeling, and Thomas Weiss (2012). *Passenger Fares for Overseas Travel in the 19th and 20th Centuries.* Economic History Association, www.eh.net/eha/wp-content/uploads/2013/11/Weissetal.pdf.

15. UNWTO (2019). "International Tourist Arrivals." United Nations World Tourism Organization, https://ourworldindata.org/tourism.

16. Edward L. Glaeser and Janet E. Kohlhase (2003). *Cities, Regions and the Decline of Transport Costs.* Working Paper 9886, National Bureau of Economic Research, www.nber.org/papers/w9886.

17. Bureau of the Census (1908). *Earnings of Wage Earners, Census of Manufactures: 1905.* US Department of Commerce and Labor, https://babel.hathi trust.org/cgi/pt?id=nnc1.cu56779232&view=1up&seq=1.

18. David S. Johnson, John M. Rogers, and Lucilla Tan (2001). "A Century of Family Budgets in the United States." *Monthly Labor Review.* May, pp. 28–46, www.bls.gov/opub/mlr/2001/05/art3full.pdf.

19. BLS (various years). *Consumer Expenditures.* Bureau of Labor Statistics, www .bls.gov/cex; Statistics Canada (2019). *Survey of Household Spending,* www .statcan.gc.ca/eng/survey/household/3508.

20. G. J. Gabbe and Gregory Pierce (2016). "Hidden Costs and Deadweight Losses: Bundled Parking and Residential Rents in the Metropolitan United States." *Housing Policy Debate*. https://.doi.org/10.1080/10511482.2016.120 5647. Also see, "The Hidden Costs of Bundled Parking." *Access Magazine*. 2017, www.accessmagazine.org/spring-2017/the-hidden-cost-of-bundled-park ing; Jesse London and Clark Williams-Derry (2013). *Who Pays for Parking? How the Oversupply of Parking Undermines Housing Affordability*. Sightline Institute, www.sightline.org/research_item/who-pays-for-parking/.

21. NHTS (2017), Table 27. *Summary of Travel Trends*. National Household Travel Survey, USDOT; at https://nhts.ornl.gov/assets/2017_nhts_summary _travel_trends.pdf.

22. Paul J. Tranter (2004). *Effective Speeds: Car Costs are Slowing Us Down*. University of New South Wales, for the Australian Greenhouse Office, http://citeseerx .ist.psu.edu/viewdoc/download?doi=10.1.1.576.1031&rep=rep1&type=pdf.

23. Henry David Thoreau made a similar argument in *Walden* when he pointed out that the fare for the thirty-mile train ride to Fitchburg would require about a day of labor, and so concludes that walking is actually faster overall. He concluded, "We do not ride on the railroad; it rides upon us."

24. Eurostat (2019). "Structure of Consumption Expenditure by Income Quintile." http://appsso.eurostat.ec.europa.eu/nui/show.do?dataset=hbs_str_t22 3&lang=en.

25. BLS (2019). "Consumer Expenditures." Bureau of Labor Statistics, www.bls .gov/news.release/cesan.nr0.htm.

26. FHWA (2018). "Table HF10," *Highway Statistics*. Federal Highway Administration, www.fhwa.dot.gov/policyinformation/statistics/2016/hf10 .cfm.

27. Eric Scharnhorst (2018). "Quantified Parking: Comprehensive Parking Inventories for Five U.S. Cities." Research Institute for Housing America Special Report, Mortgage Bankers Association, www.mba.org/Documents/18806_Re search_RIHA_Parking_Report%20(1).pdf.

28. Jacob Gonzalez (2019). "Parking Structure Cost Outlook." WGI, https://wginc .com/parking-outlook.

29. Todd Litman (2019). "Parking Costs." *Transportation Cost and Benefit Analysis*. Victoria Transport Policy Institute, www.vtpi.org/tca.

30. Patrick Balducci and Joseph Stowers (2008). *State Highway Cost Allocation Studies: A Synthesis of Highway Practice*. NCHRP Synthesis 378, www.nap.edu /catalog/14178/state-highway-cost-allocation-studies.

31. Chad Frederick, William Riggs, and John Hans Gilderbloom (2017). "Commute Mode Diversity and Public Health: A Multivariate Analysis of 148 US Cities." *International Journal of Sustainable Transportation*. https://doi.org /10.1080/15568318.2017.1321705.

32. A. Mackay et al. (2019). "Association Between Driving Time and Unhealthy Lifestyles." *Journal of Public Health* 41(3), pp. 527–34 (https://doi.org/10 .1093/pubmed/fdy155); Reid Ewing et al. (2014). "Relationship Between Urban Sprawl and Physical Activity, Obesity, and Morbidity—Update and Re-

finement." *Health & Place 26*, March, pp. 118–26, https://doi.org/10.1016 /j.healthplace.2013.12.008.

33. Shima Hamidi et al. (2018). "Associations between Urban Sprawl and Life Expectancy in the United States." *International Journal of Environmental Research and Public Health.15*(5), https://doi.org/10.3390/ijerph15050861.

34. Mauricio Avendano and Ichiro Kawachi (2014). "Why do Americans Have Shorter Life Expectancy and Worse Health than do People in Other High-Income Countries?" *Annual Review of Public Health 35*, pp. 307–25, https://doi.org/10.1146/annurev-publhealth-032013-182411.

35. EEA (2016). *Explaining Road Transport Emissions: A Non-Technical Guide*. European Environment Agency, www.eea.europa.eu/publications/explaining -road-transport-emissions.

36. UCS (2018). *Cars, Trucks, Buses and Air Pollution*. Union of Concerned Scientists, www.ucsusa.org/resources/cars-trucks-buses-and-air-pollution.

37. ALA (2017). *Living Near Highways and Air Pollution*. American Lung Association, www.lung.org/clean-air/outdoors/who-is-at-risk/highways.

38. Fabio Caiazzo et al. (2013). "Air Pollution and Early Deaths in the United States. Part I: Quantifying the Impact of Major Sectors in 2005." *Atmospheric Environment 79*, pp. 198–208, https://doi.org/10.1016/j.atmosenv.2013.05.081.

39. USEPA (2020). *Inventory of U.S. Greenhouse Gas Emissions and Sinks: 1990–2018*. US Environmental Protection Agency, www.epa.gov/ghgemissions/inventory-us-greenhouse-gas-emissions-and-sinks-1990-2018.

40. Richard Weller (2018). "New Maps Show How Urban Sprawl Threatens the World's Remaining Biodiversity." *The Dirt*, https://dirt.asla.org/2018/02 /06/new-maps-show-how-urban-sprawl-threatens-the-worlds-remaining -biodiversity/.

41. Chester Arnold and James Gibbons (1996). "Impervious Surface Coverage: The Emergence of a Key Environmental Indicator." *American Planning Association Journal 62*(2), Spring, pp. 243–58, www.esf.edu/cue/documents /Arnold-Gibbons_ImperviousSurfaceCoverage_1996.pdf.

42. Mikayla Bouchard (2015). "Transportation Emerges as Crucial to Escaping Poverty." *New York Times*, www.nytimes.com/2015/05/07/upshot/transportation-emerges-as-crucial-to-escaping-poverty.html.

43. Miles Brothers (1906). *A Trip Down Market Street*. YouTube, www.youtube .com/watch?v=8Q5Nur642BU.

44. Ricardo Baños (1908). *A Ride through Barcelona 101 Years Ago*. Flixxy, www .flixxy.com/barcelona-spain-1908.htm.

45. Joseph Stromberg (2015). "The Forgotten History of How Automakers Invented the Crime of 'Jaywalking.'" VOX, www.vox.com/2015/1/15/755 1873/jaywalking-history.

46. APTA (1969–1970). *Transit Fact Book*. https://www.apta.com/wp-content /uploads/Resources/resources/statistics/Documents/FactBook/APTA _1969-1970_Transit_Fact_Book.pdf.

47. Jonathan English (2018). "Why Public Transportation Works Better Outside the U.S." Bloomberg City Lab, https://bloom.bg/3lqRN6Q.

48. Joseph Stromberg (2016). "Highways Gutted American Cities. So Why Did They Build Them?" VOX, www.vox.com/2015/5/14/8605917/highways -interstate-cities-history.

49. Rick Brown (2018). "Interstate Injustice: Plowing Through Minority Neighborhoods." Panethos, https://panethos.wordpress.com/2018/04/07/inter state-injustice-plowing-highways-through-minority-neighborhoods/.

50. Brinkman and Lin (2019). *Freeway Revolts!*

51. Susan Handy (2020). *What California Gains from Reducing Car Dependence.* National Center for Sustainable Transportation, https://escholarship.org /uc/item/0hk0h610.

52. Marlon G. Boarnet (2013). "The Declining Role of the Automobile and the Re-Emergence of Place in Urban Transportation: The Past Will be Prologue." *Regional Science Policy and Practice 5*, pp. 237–53, https://doi.org /10.1111/rsp3.12007.

Chapter 3

1. ADB (2009). *Changing Course: A New Paradigm for Sustainable Urban Transport.* Asian Development Bank, www.adb.org/publications/changing-course -new-paradigm-sustainable-urban-transport.

2. Michelle DeRobertis et al. (2014). "Changing the Paradigm of Traffic Impact Studies: How Typical Traffic Studies Inhibit Sustainable Transportation." *ITE Journal.* May, pp. 30–35, http://transportchoice.org/wp-content/uploads /2014/05/DeRobertis_et_al_ChangingTheParadigm-May_2014_ITE Journal.pdf.

3. Brookings Institution (2016). *Moving to Access Initiative.* Brookings Institution, https://brook.gs/3kxTpud.

4. ITF (2019). *Improving Transport Planning and Investment Through the Use of Accessibility Indicators.* International Transport Forum, www.itf-oecd.org /transport-planning-investment-accessibility-indicators.

5. NYCDOT (2012). *Measuring the Street: New Metrics for 21st Century Streets.* New York City Department of Transportation, https://on.nyc.gov /2C5Y5Xf.

6. NAR (2017). *National Community Preference Survey.* National Association of Realtors, www.nar.realtor/reports/nar-2017-community-preference-survey.

7. Hanna Hüging, Kain Glensor, and Oliver Lah (2014). *The TIDE Impact Assessment Method for Urban Transport Innovations: A Handbook for Local Practitioners.* Transport Innovation Deployment for Europe Project, https://www .eltis.org/sites/default/files/trainingmaterials/tide-assessment-handbook -lite.pdf

8.   DfT (2006–2018). *Transport Analysis Guidance.* UK Department for Transport, www.gov.uk/guidance/transport-analysis-guidance-tag.

9.   Ricardo-AEA (2014). *Update of the Handbook on External Costs of Transport Final Report.* European Commission, https://ec.europa.eu/transport/sites/transport/files/themes/sustainable/studies/doc/2014-handbook-external-costs-transport.pdf.

10. NZTA (2010–2017). *Economic Evaluation Manual,* Volumes 1 and 2. New Zealand Transport Agency, www.nzta.govt.nz/resources/economic-evaluation-manual and www.nzta.govt.nz/assets/resources/economic-evaluation-manual/volume-2/docs/eem2-july-2010.pdf.

11. Todd Litman (2009). *Transportation Cost and Benefit Analysis.* Victoria Transport Policy Institute, www.vtpi.org/tdm.

12. Tony Dutzik, Gideon Weissman, and Phineas Baxandall (2015). *Who Pays for Roads? How the "Users Pay" Myth Gets in the Way of Solving America's Transportation Problems.* US PIRG, https://uspirg.org/sites/pirg/files/reports/Who%20Pays%20for%20Roads%20vUS.pdf.

13. Eric Scharnhorst (2018). *Quantified Parking: Comprehensive Parking Inventories for Five U.S. Cities.* Research Institute for Housing America Special Report, Mortgage Bankers Association, www.mba.org/Documents/18806_Research_RIHA_Parking_Report%20(1).pdf.

14. Kara Kockelman et al. (2013). *The Economics of Transportation Systems: A Reference for Practitioners.* TxDOT Project 0-6628, University of Texas at Austin. www.utexas.edu/research/ctr/pdf_reports/0_6628_P1.pdf.

15. Eric Bruun and Vukan Vuchic (1995). "The Time-Area Concept: Development, Meaning and Applications." *Transportation Research Record 1499,* pp. 95–104.

16. Todd Litman (2014). *Economically Optimal Transport Prices and Markets: What Would Happen if Rational Policies Prevailed?* International Transportation Economic Development Conference, Dallas, Texas, www.vtpi.org/ITED_optimal.pdf.

17. CARB (2014). *Research on Effects of Transportation and Land Use–Related Policies.* California Air Resources Board, https://ww2.arb.ca.gov/our-work/programs/sustainable-communities-program/research-effects-transportation-and-land-use.

18. CARB (2014). *Effects of Transportation and Land Use–Related Policies.*

19. Allen Greenberg and Jay Evans (2017). *Comparing Greenhouse Gas Reductions and Legal Implementation Possibilities for Pay-to-Save Transportation Price-Shifting Strategies and EPA's Clean Power Plan.* Presented to the Union of Concerned Scientists, www.vtpi.org/G&E_GHG.pdf; slideshow at www.vtpi.org/Greenberg%26Evans_PAYD_UCS_30Aug2017.pdf.

20. FHWA (2009). *Economics: Pricing, Demand, and Economic Efficiency: A Primer.* Office of Transportation Management, Federal Highway Administration, https://ops.fhwa.dot.gov/publications/fhwahop08041/fhwahop08041.pdf.

21. Brianne Eby, Martha Roskowski, and Robert Puentes (2020). *Congestion Pricing in the United States: Principles for Developing a Viable Program to Advance Sustainability and Equity Goals*. Eno Center for Transportation, https://www.enotrans.org/eno-resources/enocongestionpricing/.

22. Justine Sears (2014). *Least-Cost Transportation Planning*. Vermont Energy Investment Corporation, www.veic.org/clients-results/reports/least-cost-transportation-planning.

23. Gregory H. Shill (2020). "Should Law Subsidize Driving?" *New York University Law Review 498*. University of Iowa Legal Studies Research Paper No. 2019-03, https://doi.org/10.2139/ssrn.3345366.

24. SSTI (2018). *Modernizing Mitigation: A Demand-Centered Approach*. State Smart Transportation Initiative and the Mayors Innovation Project, https://ssti.us/wp-content/uploads/sites/1303/2020/05/Modernizing_Mitigation_2018.pdf.

25. Todd Litman (2014). *Economically Optimal Transport Prices and Markets: What Would Happen if Rational Policies Prevailed?* Presented at the International Transportation Economic Development Conference, April 9–11, 2014, Dallas, Texas, www.vtpi.org/sotpm.pdf.

26. ACEEE (2019). *Sustainable Transportation Planning*. American Council for an Energy Efficient Economy, https://database.aceee.org/city/sustainable-transportation-planning.

27. GOPR (2018). *On Evaluating Transportation Impacts in CEQA*. Governor's Office of Planning and Research, http://opr.ca.gov/ceqa/updates/sb-743.

28. WSL (2008). *Adoption of Statewide Goals to Reduce Annual Per Capita Vehicle Miles Traveled by 2050*. Washington State Legislature, https://apps.leg.wa.gov/RCW/default.aspx?cite=47.01.440.

29. Amy E. Lee and Susan L. Handy (2018). "Leaving Level-of-Service Behind: The Implications of a Shift to VMT Impact Metrics." *Research in Transportation Business and Management 29*, pp. 14–29, https://doi.org/10.1016/j.rtbm.2018.02.003.

30. Michelle Byars, Yishu Wei, and Susan Handy (2017). *State-Level Strategies for Reducing Vehicle Miles of Travel*. University of California Institute of Transportation Studies, www.ucits.org/research-project/strategies-for-reducing-vehicle-miles-traveled-vmt-synthesizing-the-evidence/.

31. FHWA (2014). *Nonmotorized Transportation Pilot Program: Continued Progress in Developing Walking and Bicycling Networks—May 2014 Report*. John A Volpe National Transportation Systems Center, USDOT, www.fhwa.dot.gov/environment/bicycle_pedestrian/ntpp/2014_report/hep14035.pdf.

32. King County (2019). *Commute Trip Reduction (CTR)*, https://kingcounty.gov/depts/transportation/metro/employer-programs/commute-trip-reduction.aspx.

33. Erick Trickey (2019). "Has Seattle Found the Solution to Driving Alone to Work?" *Politico*, https://politi.co/3lnj9Ld.

34. Stanford University Transportation, http://transportation.stanford.edu.

35. SUTP (2019). *Mobilizing Minds: Mobility Management at Universities.* Sustainable Urban Transport Program, www.indiaenvironmentportal.org.in/files /file/GIZ_SUTP_Mobility-Management-at-Universities.pdf.

36. John L. Renne (2013). "The Pent-Up Demand for Transit-Oriented Development and Its Role in Reducing Oil Dependence." In John L. Renne and Billy Fields (eds), *Transport Beyond Oil: Policy Choices for a Multimodal Future.* Washington, DC: Island Press.

37. Daniel Herriges (2020). "7 Rules for Creating '15-Minute Neighborhoods.'" Strong Towns, www.strongtowns.org/journal/2019/9/6/7-rules-for-cre ating-15-minute-neighborhoods.

38. Green Vancouver (2030). *Climate Emergency Action Plan.* City of Vancouver, https://vancouver.ca/green-vancouver/vancouvers-climate-emergency.aspx.

39. Robert J. Schneider, Susan L. Handy, and Kevan Shafizadeh (2014). "Trip Generation for Smart Growth Projects." *ACCESS* 45, pp. 10–15, www.access magazine.org/fall-2014/trip-generation-smart-growth-projects/.

40. Todd Litman (2016). *Selling Smart Growth.* Victoria Transport Policy Institute, www.vtpi.org/ssg.pdf.

Chapter 4

1. Donald Shoup (2005). *The High Cost of Free Parking.* New York: Planners Press.

2. For more analysis of these costs see Todd Litman (2019). *Transportation Cost and Benefit Analysis.* Victoria Transport Policy Institute, www.vtpi.org/tca.

3. DfT (various years). *Transport Analysis Guidance.* UK Department for Transport, www.gov.uk/guidance/transport-analysis-guidance-webtag.

4. ATAP (2017). *Australian Transport Assessment and Planning Guidelines.* ATAP Steering Committee Secretariat. Australia Department of Infrastructure and Regional Development, www.atap.gov.au.

5. NZTA (2017). *Economic Evaluation Manual, Vols 1 and 2.* New Zealand Transport Agency, https://www.nzta.govt.nz/resources/economic-evaluation -manual and www.nzta.govt.nz/assets/resources/economic-evaluation-man ual/volume-2/docs/eem2-july-2010.pdf.

6. EU (2014). *Guide to Cost-Benefit Analysis of Investment Projects: Economic Appraisal Tool for Cohesion Policy 2014–2020.* European Commission, https: //ec.europa.eu/regional_policy/sources/docgener/studies/pdf/cba_guide .pdf.

7. Todd Litman (2019). *Transportation Cost and Benefit Analysis.* Victoria Transport Policy Institute, www.vtpi.org/tca.

8. Todd Litman (2020). *Evaluating Transportation Equity.* Victoria Transport Policy Institute, www.vtpi.org/equity.pdf.

9. Michelle DeRobertis et al. (2014). "Changing the Paradigm of Traffic Impact Studies: How Typical Traffic Studies Inhibit Sustainable Transportation." *ITE Journal.* May, pp. 30–35, https://trid.trb.org/view.aspx?id=1311221.

10. Project Drawdown. https://drawdown.org.

11. Kevin Fang and Jamey Volker (2017). *Cutting Greenhouse Gas Emissions Is Only the Beginning: A Literature Review of the Co-Benefits of Reducing Vehicle Miles Traveled.* National Center for Sustainable Transportation, University of California, Davis, https://escholarship.org/uc/item/4h5494vr.

12. Alexis Corning-Padilla and Gregory Rowangould (2020). "Sustainable and Equitable Financing for Sidewalk Maintenance." *Cities, 107,* https://doi.org /10.1016/j.cities.2020.102874.

Chapter 5

1. Rasheq Zarif, Ben Kelman, and Derek M. Pankratz (2019). *Small Is Beautiful. Making Micromobility Work for Citizens, Cities, and Service Providers.* Deloitte, www2.deloitte.com/content/dam/insights/us/articles/5000_small-is -beautiful/DI_Small-is-beautiful.pdf.

2. Todd Litman (2019). *Evaluating Active Transport Benefits and Costs.* Victoria Transport Policy Institute, www.vtpi.org/nmt-tdm.pdf.

3. Jan Gehl (2010). *Cities for People.* Washington, DC: Island Press.

4. ARUP (2020). *Cities Alive: Towards a Walking World.* London: ARUP, www .arup.com/perspectives/publications/research/section/cities-alive-towards -a-walking-world.

5. SGA (2020). "What Are Complete Streets?" Smart Growth America, https: //smartgrowthamerica.org/category/complete-streets.

6. Madeline Brozen et al. (2014). *Exploration and Implications of Multimodal Street Performance Metrics: What's a Passing Grade?* UCTC-FR-2014-09, University of California Transportation Center, www.lewis.ucla.edu/wp-content /uploads/sites/2/2014/09/EXPLORATION-AND-IMPLICATIONS-OF -MULTIMODAL-STREET-PERFORMANCE-METRICS.pdf.

7. QT (ND). *Reducing Conflict between Bicycle Riders and Pedestrians.* Queenland Transport, www.tmr.qld.gov.au/-/media/Travelandtransport/Cycling /Bike-user-guide/Technical-information/C2_Reducing_conflict_between _bicycle_riders_and_pedestrians.pdf?la=en.

8. J. Richard Kuzmyak and Jennifer Dill (2012). "Walking and Bicycling in the United States: The Who, What, Where, and Why." *TR News* 280. May–June, http://onlinepubs.trb.org/onlinepubs/trnews/trnews280www.pdf.

9. Torsha Bhattacharya, Kevin Mills, and Tiffany Mulally (2019). *Active Transportation Transforms America: The Case for Increased Public Investment in Walking and Biking Connectivity.* Rails-to-Trails Conservancy, www.railsto trails.org/media/847675/activetransport_2019-report_finalreduced.pdf.

10. NAR (2017). *National Community Preference Surveys.* National Association of Realtors, www.nar.realtor/reports/nar-community-and-transportation-pref erences-surveys.

11. USDOT (2015). *Transportation and Health Tool.* US Department of Transportation, www.transportation.gov/transportation-health-tool.

12. NACTO (2020). *Streets for Pandemic Response and Recovery.* National Association of City Transportation Officials, https://nacto.org/publication/streets -for-pandemic-response-recovery.

13. Laura Sandt, Tabitha Combs, and Jesse Cohn (2016). *Pursuing Equity in Pedestrian and Bicycle Planning.* US Federal Highway Administration, www.fhwa.dot.gov/environment/bicycle_pedestrian/resources/equity _paper.

14. LAW (2013). *The New Majority: Pedaling Towards Equity.* League of American Bicyclists, www.bikeleague.org/sites/default/files/equity_report.pdf.

15. Reid Ewing and Shima Hamidi (2015). *How Affordable Is HUD Affordable Housing?* National Institute for Transportation & Communities, www.tand fonline.com/doi/abs/10.1080/10511482.2015.1123753.

16. ABW (2018). *Bicycling and Walking in the U.S.: Benchmarking Reports.* Alliance for Biking & Walking, http://bikingandwalkingbenchmarks.org.

17. James F. Sallis et al. (2015), "Co-Benefits of Designing Communities for Active Living: An Exploration of Literature," *International Journal of Behavioral Nutrition and Physical Activity 12*(30), https://doi.org/10.1186/s12966 -015-0188-2.

18. ACEEE (2019). *Mode Shift.* American Council for an Energy Efficient Economy, https://database.aceee.org/city/mode-shift.

19. Collin Roughton et al. (2012). *Creating Walkable and Bikeable Communities: A User Guide to Developing Pedestrian and Bicycle Master Plans.* Center for Transportation Studies at Portland State University, https://ppms.trec.pdx.edu /media/project_files/IBPI%20Master%20Plan%20Handbook%20FINAL .pdf.

20. Sam Swartz (2012). *Steps to a Walkable Community: A Guide for Citizens, Planners, and Engineers.* America Walks, www.americawalks.org/walksteps.

21. NACTO (2016). *Global Street Design Guide.* National Association of City Transportation Officials, https://globaldesigningcities.org/publication/global -street-design-guide/.

22. OF (2017). *Outdoor Participation Report.* Outdoor Foundation, https: //outdoorindustry.org/wp-content/uploads/2017/05/2017-Outdoor -Recreation-Participation-Report_FINAL.pdf.

23. Clinical Committee (2019). *Biking vs Driving vs Taking the Train to Work.* Visualized Health, www.clearvuehealth.com/b/biking-driving-commute/.

24. NAR (2017). *National Community Preference Survey.*

25. Maaza C. Mekuria, Peter G. Furth, and Hilary Nixon (2012). *Low-Stress Bicycling and Network Connectivity.* Mineta Transportation Institute, https://trans web.sjsu.edu/research/low-stress-bicycling-and-network-connectivity.

26. Walkable Communities, Inc. "Walkable Communities Library." www.walkable .org/library.htm.

27. Bhattacharya, Mills, and Mulally (2019). *Active Transportation Transforms America.*

28. CPSTF (2017). *Physical Activity: Built Environment Approaches Combining Transportation System Interventions with Land Use and Environmental Design.* US Center for Disease Control, *The Community Guide,* www.thecom munityguide.org/findings/physical-activity-built-environment-approaches.

29. Hongwei Dong (2020). *The Geographic Disparities in Transportation-Related Physical Activity in the United States: An Analysis of the 2017 NHTS Data.* Mineta Transportation Institute, https://transweb.sjsu.edu/sites/default/files /1912-Dong-Geographic-Disparities-Transportation-Related-Physical-Ac tivity-US.pdf.

30. Ralph Buehler (2016). *Moving Toward Active Transportation: How Policies Can Encourage Walking and Bicycling.* Active Living Research, https://activeliv ingresearch.org/sites/activelivingresearch.org/files/ALR_Review_Ac tiveTransport_January2016.pdf.

31. Jessica Y. Guo and Sasanka Gandavarapu (2010). "An Economic Evaluation of Health-Promotive Built Environment Changes." *Preventive Medicine 50* (Supplement 1), January, pp. S44–S49, https://doi.org/10.1016/j.ypmed.2009 .08.019.

32. Aslak Fyhri and Hanne Beate Sundfør (2020). "Do People Who Buy E-bikes Cycle More?" *Transportation Research Part D, 86,* https://doi.org/10 .1016/j.trd.2020.102422.

33. Jacob Mason, Lew Fulton, and Zane McDonald (2015). *A Global High Shift Cycling Scenario: The Potential for Dramatically Increasing Bicycle and E-bike Use in Cities Around the World.* ITDP and the University of California, https://itdpdotorg.wpengine.com/wp-content/uploads/2015/11/A -Global-High-Shift-Cycling-Scenario_Nov-2015.pdf.

34. Michael McQueen, John MacArthur, and Christopher Cherry (2020). "The E-Bike Potential: Estimating Regional E-bike Impacts on Greenhouse Gas Emissions." *Transportation Research Part D, 87,* https://doi.org/10.1016/j .trd.2020.102482.

35. Dominik Bucher et al. (2019). "Energy and Greenhouse Gas Emission Reduction Potentials Resulting from Different Commuter Electric Bicycle Adoption Scenarios in Switzerland." *Renewable and Sustainable Energy Reviews, 114,* https://doi.org/10.1016/j.rser.2019.109298.

36. Christopher Standen (2018). "The Value of Slow Travel: An Econometric Method for Valuing the User Benefits of Active Transport Infrastructure." (PhD thesis, University of Sydney), https://ses.library.usyd.edu.au/handle /2123/17914.

37. Talia Shadwell (2017). "'Paying to Stay Safe': Why Women Don't Walk as Much as Men." *The Guardian,* www.theguardian.com/inequality/2017/oct /11/paying-to-stay-safe-why-women-dont-walk-as-much-as-men.

38. Shigehiro Oishi, Minkyung Koo, and Nicholas R. Buttrick (2018). "The Socioecological Psychology of Upward Social Mobility." *American Psychologist, 74*(7), 751–63, https://doi.org/10.1037/amp0000422.
39. Alexis Corning-Padilla and Gregory Rowangould (2020). "Sustainable and Equitable Financing for Sidewalk Maintenance." *Cities, 107*, https://doi.org/10.1016/j.cities.2020.102874.
40. ABW (2018). *Bicycling and Walking in the U.S.*
41. Maggie L. Grabow et al. (2011). "Air Quality and Exercise-Related Health Benefits from Reduced Car Travel in the Midwestern United States." *Environmental Health Perspectives*, http://dx.doi.org/10.1289/ehp.1103440.
42. Thorsten Koska and Frederic Rudolph (2016). *The Role of Walking and Cycling in Reducing Congestion: A Portfolio of Measures*. FLOW Project, http://h2020-flow.eu/uploads/tx_news/FLOW_REPORT_-_Portfolio_of_Measures_v_06_web.pdf.
43. Sara Zimmerman et al. (2015). *At the Intersection of Active Transportation and Equity*. Safe Routes to Schools, www.saferoutespartnership.org/sites/default/files/resource_files/at-the-intersection-of-active-transportation-and-equity.pdf.
44. Rune Elvik (2009). "The Non-Linearity of Risk and the Promotion of Environmentally Sustainable Transport." *Crash Analysis and Prevention, 41*(4), pp. 849–55.
45. WHO (2018). "Physical Activity." World Health Organization, www.who.int/news-room/fact-sheets/detail/physical-activity.
46. Carlos A. Celis-Morales et al. (2017). "Association Between Active Commuting and Incident Cardiovascular Disease, Cancer, and Mortality: Prospective Cohort Study." *BMJ*, https://doi.org/10.1136/bmj.j1456.
47. Adam Martin, Yevgeniy Goryakin, and Marc Suhrcke (2014). "Does Active Commuting Improve Psychological Wellbeing? Longitudinal Evidence from Eighteen Waves of the British Household Panel Survey." *Preventive Medicine*, www.sciencedirect.com/science/article/pii/S0091743514003144.
48. Sandra Caballero and Philippe Rapin (2020). "COVID-19 Made Cities More Bike-Friendly—Here's How To Keep Them That Way." World Economic Forum, www.weforum.org/agenda/2020/06/covid-19-made-cities-more-bike-friendly-here-s-how-to-keep-them-that-way/.
49. USDOT (2020). "Safe Routes to School Programs." Department of Transportation, www.transportation.gov/mission/health/Safe-Routes-to-School-Programs.
50. "Shared-Use Mobility Center." https://sharedusemobilitycenter.org.
51. NACTO (2018). *Bike Share and Shared Micromobility Initiative*. National Association of City Transportation Officials, https://nacto.org/program/bike-share-initiative.
52. Saki Aono (2019). *Identifying Best Practices for Mobility Hubs*. UBC Sustainability, https://sustain.ubc.ca/sites/default/files/Sustainability%20Schol

ars/2018_Sustainability_Scholars/Reports/2018-71%20Identifying%20
Best%20Practices%20for%20Mobility%20Hubs_Aono.pdf.

53. Alexandros Nikitas (2019). "How to Save Bike-Sharing: An Evidence-Based Survival Toolkit for Policy-Makers and Mobility Providers." *Sustainability, 11*, https://doi.org/10.3390/su11113206.

54. SUMC (2016). "Shared-Use Mobility Toolkit for Cities." Shared-Use Mobility Center, https://sharedusemobilitycenter.org.

55. Christopher Moon-Miklaucic et al. (2019). "The Evolution of Bike Sharing: 10 Questions on the Emergence of New Technologies, Opportunities, and Risks." World Resources Institute, www.wri.org/publication/evolution-bike-sharing.

56. T. Donna Chen and Kara Kockelman (2016). "Carsharing's Life-cycle Impacts on Energy Use and Greenhouse Gas Emissions." *Transportation Research Part D, 47*, pp. 276–84, https:/doi.org/10.1016/j.trd.2016.05.012.

57. Susan Shaheen and Nelson Chan (2015). *Mobility and the Shared Economy: Impact Synopsis*. Transportation Sustainability Research Center, http://in novativemobility.org/wp-content/uploads/Innovative-Mobility-Industry -Outlook_SM-Spring-2015.pdf.

58. Amanda Merck (2020). "6 Ways to Correct Bike Share's Social Equity Prob- lem." SaludAmerica, https://salud-america.org/6-ways-to-correct-bike-shares -social-equity-problem/.

59. SUMC (2019). *Equity and Shared Mobility Services: Working with the Pri- vate Sector to Meet Equity Objectives*. Shared-Use Mobility Center, https://share dusemobilitycenter.org/wp-content/uploads/2019/12/EquityShared MobilityServices-FINAL.pdf.

60. TRB (2020). *Shared Mobility and the Transformation of Public Transit*. Trans- portation Research Board, https://doi.org/10.17226/23578.

61. Nathan McNeil et al. (2017). *Evaluating Efforts to Improve the Equity of Bike Share Systems*. Transportation Research and Education Center, https://trec.pdx .edu/research/project/884/Evaluating_Efforts_to_Improve_the_Equity_of _Bike_Share_Systems.

62. SUMC (2020). "Learning Module: Microtransit." Shared-Use Mobility Center, https://learn.sharedusemobilitycenter.org/learning_module/microtransit/.

63. Susan Pike and Raiza Pilatwosky Gruner (2020). *Ridehailing, Uncertainty, and Sustainable Transportation: How Transportation Stakeholders Are Respond- ing to the Unknowns Surrounding Ridehailing*. National Center for Sustainable Transportation, https://escholarship.org/uc/item/6q1382xd.

64. "RideGuru." https://ride.guru/content/about/meet-the-gurus.

65. Bruce Schaller (2018). *The New Automobility: Lyft, Uber and the Future of American Cities*. Schaller Consulting, www.schallerconsult.com/rideservices /automobility.pdf.

66. Alejandro Tirachini (2019). "Ride-Hailing, Travel Behaviour and Sustainable Mobility: An International Review." *Transportation*, https://doi.org/10.1007 /s11116-019-10070-2.

67. Schaller (2018). *New Automobility.*

68. Angie Schmitt (2018). "The Story of 'Micro Transit' Is Consistent, Dismal Failure." Streetsblog USA, https://usa.streetsblog.org/2018/06/26/the-story-of-micro-transit-is-consistent-dismal-failure/.

69. RideGuru. https://ride.guru.

70. John Manuel Barrios, Yael V. Hochberg, and Hanyi Yi (2019). *The Cost of Convenience: Ridesharing and Traffic Fatalities.* Chicago Booth Research Paper 27, https://doi.org/10.2139/ssrn.3259965.

71. Lawrence Mishel (2018). *Uber and the Labor Market.* Economic Policy Institute, www.epi.org/publication/uber-and-the-labor-market-uber-drivers-compensation-wages-and-the-scale-of-uber-and-the-gig-economy/.

72. SUMC (2020). "Learning Module: Microtransit."

73. Schaller (2018). *New Automobility.*

74. ITF (2016). *The Shared-Use City: Managing the Curb.* International Transport Forum, www.itf-oecd.org/sites/default/files/docs/shared-use-city-managing-curb.pdf.

75. Venkat Viswanathan, Alexander Bills, and Shashank Sripad (2020). "The Road to Electric Vehicles with Lower Sticker Prices than Gas Cars." *Government Technology*, www.govtech.com/fs/transportation/The-Road-to-Electric-Vehicles-with-Lower-Sticker-Prices-than-Gas-Cars--Battery-Costs-Explained.html.

76. EEI (2019). *Electric Vehicle Sales: Facts & Figures.* Edison Electric Institute, www.eei.org/issuesandpolicy/electrictransportation/Documents/FINAL_EV_Sales_Update_April2019.pdf.

77. Sandra Wappelhorst (2020). *The End of the Road? An Overview of Combustion-engine Car Phase-Out Announcements.* International Council for Clean Transportation, https://theicct.org/sites/default/files/publications/Combustion-engine-phase-out-briefing-may11.2020.pdf.

78. Michael Sivak and Brandon Schoettle (2018). *Relative Costs of Driving Electric and Gasoline Vehicles in the Individual U.S. States.* Sustainable Worldwide Transportation, http://umich.edu/~umtriswt/PDF/SWT-2018-1.pdf.

79. Assuming a -0.2 to -0.4 long-run elasticity of vehicle travel with respect to perceived operating costs, based on Joshua Linn (2013). *The Rebound Effect for Passenger Vehicles.* Discussion Paper 13-19. Resources for the Future, www.rff.org/publications/working-papers/the-rebound-effect-for-passenger-vehicles/.

80. MIT (2020). *Insights into Future Mobility.* Massachusetts Institute of Technology, http://energy.mit.edu/research/mobilityofthefuture/.

81. Edmunds (2019). "The True Cost of Powering an Electric Car." https://edmu.in/2CT1k5s.

82. David Reighmuth (2020). "Are Electric Vehicles Really Better for the Climate? Yes. Here's Why." Union of Concerned Scientists, https://blog.ucsusa.org/dave-reichmuth/are-electric-vehicles-really-better-for-the-climate-yes-heres-why.

83. Todd Litman (2013). "Full Cost Analysis of Petroleum." In John Renne and Billy Fields (eds), *Transport Beyond Oil: Policy Choices for a Multimodal Future*. Washington, DC: Island Press.

84. EA (2020). "Tyres not Tailpipes." Emissions Analytics, www.emissions analytics.com/news/2020/1/28/tyres-not-tailpipe.

85. Cameron Roberts (2020). "There Aren't Enough Batteries to Electrify All Cars—Focus on Trucks and Buses Instead." *The Conversation*, https://the conversation.com/there-arent-enough-batteries-to-electrify-all-cars-focus -on-trucks-and-buses-instead-142545.

86. Todd Litman (2020). *Autonomous Vehicle Implementation Predictions: Implications for Transport Planning*. www.vtpi.org/avip.pdf.

87. John J. Leonard, David A. Mindell, and Erik L. Stayton (2020). *Autonomous Vehicles, Mobility, and Employment Policy: The Roads Ahead*. MIT Work of the Future, https://workofthefuture.mit.edu/research-post/autonomous -vehicles-mobility-and-employment-policy-the-roads-ahead/.

88. Leonard, Mindell, and Stayton (2020). *Autonomous Vehicles, Mobility, and Employment Policy*.

89. Litman (2020). *Autonomous Vehicle Implementation Predictions*.

90. Meredith Broussard (2018). "The Dirty Truth Coming for Self-Driving Cars: Trash. Odors. Bodily Fluids. Will Autonomous Rideshares be Ready for our Mess?" *Slate*, https://slate.me/2Ls9IrI.

91. Caroline Rodier (2018). *Travel Effects and Associated Greenhouse Gas Emissions of Automated Vehicles*. UC Davis Institute for Transportation Studies, https://ncst.ucdavis.edu/research-product/travel-effects-and-associated -greenhouse-gas-emissions-automated-vehicles.

92. Morteza Taiebat, Samuel Stolper, and Ming Xu (2019). "Forecasting the Impact of Connected and Automated Vehicles on Energy Use: A Microeconomic Study of Induced Travel and Energy Rebound." *Applied Energy, 247*, pp. 297–308, https://doi.org/10.1016/j.apenergy.2019.03.174.

93. Daniel Sperling (2017). *Three Revolutions: Steering Automated, Shared, and Electric Vehicles to a Better Future*. Washington, DC: Island Press.

94. Irem Kok et al. (2017). *Rethinking Transportation 2020–2030: Disruption of Transportation and the Collapse of the Internal-Combustion Vehicle & Oil Industries*. RethinkX, www.wsdot.wa.gov/publications/fulltext/ProjectDev /PSEProgram/Disruption-of-Transportation.pdf.

95. ITF (2020). *Good to Go? Assessing the Environmental Performance of New Mobility*. International Transport Forum, www.itf-oecd.org/sites/default/files /docs/environmental-performance-new-mobility.pdf.

96. Patrick Bösch et al. (2017). *Cost-based Analysis of Autonomous Mobility Services*. Working Paper 1225, Institute for Transport Planning and Systems, www.ivt.ethz.ch/institut/vpl/publikationen/papers/1225.html.

97. ITF (2018). *Safer Roads with Automated Vehicles?* International Transport Forum, www.itf-oecd.org/sites/default/files/docs/safer-roads-automated -vehicles.pdf.

98. Altexsoft (2018). "Public Transportation Apps' APIs and Platforms: Maps, Scheduling, Trip Planning, and Mobile Ticketing." Altexsoft, www.altexsoft .com/blog/engineering/public-transportation-apps-apis-and-platforms -maps-scheduling-trip-planning-and-mobile-ticketing/.

99. Lloyd Wright (2017). *Bus Rapid Transit Planning Guide*. Institute for Transportation and Development Policy, http://www.itdp.org/microsites/bus -rapid-transit-planning-guide/https://brtguide.itdp.org.

100. "Global BRT Data." Global BRTData, http://brtdata.org.

101. EESI (2018). *Fact Sheet: High Speed Rail Development Worldwide*. Environmental and Energy Study Institute, www.eesi.org/papers/view/fact-sheet -high-speed-rail-development-worldwide.

102. Buford Furman (2014). *Automated Transit Networks (ATN): A Review of the State of the Industry and Prospects for the Future*. Mineta Transportation Institute, https://transweb.sjsu.edu/research/automated-transit-networks-atn-re view-state-industry-and-prospects-future.

103. G.B. Arrington et al. (2008). *Effects of TOD on Housing, Parking, and Travel*. Report 128, Transit Cooperative Research Program, www.trb.org/Publications /Blurbs/160307.aspx.

104. Hiroaki Suzuki, Robert Cervero, and Kanako Iuchi (2013). *Transforming Cities with Transit: Transit and Land-Use Integration for Sustainable Urban Development*. World Bank, https://doi.org/10.1596/978-0-8213-97 45-9.

105. Doug Trumm (2019). "Transit Ridership Is Flattening, but We Can Fix That." *The Urbanist*, www.theurbanist.org/2019/12/19/transit-ridership-is -flattening-but-we-can-fix-that/.

106. Conrad Zbikowski (2019). *How Houston Reimagined Its Transit Network and Increased Ridership*. Street Minnesota, https://streets.mn/2019/02/25 /how-houston-reimagined-its-transit-network-and-increased-ridership/.

107. Todd Litman (2020). *Evaluating Public Transit Benefits and Costs*. Victoria Transport Policy Institute, www.vtpi.org/tranben.pdf.

108. Maxine Joselow (2020). "There Is Little Evidence That Mass Transit Poses a Risk of Coronavirus Outbreaks." *Scientific American*, www.scientificameri can.com/article/there-is-little-evidence-that-mass-transit-poses-a-risk-of -coronavirus-outbreaks/.

109. ERTICO (2019). *Mobility as a Service (MaaS) and Sustainable Urban Mobility Planning*. ELTIS, www.eltis.org/sites/default/files/mobility_as_a_ser vice_maas_and_sustainable_urban_mobility_planning.pdf.

110. Aono (2019). *Identifying Best Practices for Mobility Hubs*

111. IT (2020). "Market Update: What's the Current State of Play in Developing Sustainable MaaS? *Intelligent Transport*, www.intelligenttransport.com /transport-webinars/98137/market-update-whats-the-current-state-of-play -in-developing-sustainable-maas/.

112. MG (2019). *A Brief History of MaaS Global, the Company behind the Whim App*. MaaS Global, https://whimapp.com/history-of-maas-global.

113. Katie Pyzyk (2019). "There's an App for That: Transit Agencies Tackle MaaS Platform Development." *Smart Cities Dive*, www.smartcitiesdive.com/news /theres-an-app-for-that-transit-agencies-tackle-maas-platform-development /557234/.

114. Johan Herrlin (2019). "The Death of Car Ownership and the Rise of MaaS." Business MaaS, www.businessmaas.com/apps/the-death-of-car-ownership -and-the-rise-of-maas/.

115. Yale Z. Wong, David A. Hensher, and Corinne Mulley (2020). "Mobility as a Service (MaaS): Charting a Future Context." *Transportation Research Part A: Policy and Practice, 131,* pp. 5–19, https://doi.org/10.1016/j.tra.2019 .09.030.

116. MA (2020). *MaaS Guide.* MaaS Alliance, https://maas.guide.

117. Neil G. Sipe and Dorina Pojani (2018). "For Mobility as a Service (Maas) to Solve Our Transport Woes, Some Things Need to Change." *The Conversation*, https://theconversation.com/for-mobility-as-a-service-maas-to-solve-our -transport-woes-some-things-need-to-change-105119.

118. "Global Workplace Analytics." Global Workplace Analytics, https://global workplaceanalytics.com.

119. Prithwiraj (Raj) Choudhury, Cirrus Foroughi, and Barbara Larson (2019). *Live and Work from Anywhere: Geographic Flexibility and Productivity Effects at the United States Patent Office.* Working Paper 19-054, Harvard Business School, https://doi.org/10.2139/ssrn.3494473.

120. Katherine Guyot and Isabel V. Sawhill (2020). "Telecommuting Will Likely Continue Long after the Pandemic." *Up Front*, Brookings Institution, https: //brook.gs/3ivORnu.

121. Matthew Dey et al. (2020). "Ability to Work From Home: Evidence from Two Surveys and Implications for the Labor Market in the COVID-19 Pandemic." *Monthly Labor Review.* US Bureau of Labor Statistics, https://doi .org/10.21916/mlr.2020.14.

122. Susan Handy, Gil Tal, and Marlon G. Boarnet (2014). *Policy Brief on the Impacts of Telecommuting Based on a Review of the Empirical Literature.* For Research on Impacts of Transportation and Land Use-Related Policies, California Air Resources Board, http://arb.ca.gov/cc/sb375/policies/poli cies.htm.

123. Lloyd Alter (2019). "How Online Shopping Is Making Congestion and Pollution Worse." *Treehugger*, www.treehugger.com/how-online-shopping -making-congestion-and-pollution-worse-4855220.

124. William O'Brien and Fereshteh Yazdani Aliabadi (2020). "Does Telecommuting Save Energy? A Critical Review of Quantitative Studies and Their Research Methods." *Energy and Buildings, 225,* https://doi.org/10.1016/j .enbuild.2020.110298.

125. Andrew Hook et al. (2020). "A Systematic Review of the Energy and Climate Impacts of Teleworking." *Environmental Research Letters*, https://iop science.iop.org/article/10.1088/1748-9326/ab8a84.

126. TBC (2019). "Frequently Asked Questions." The Boring Company, www
.boringcompany.com/faq.

127. "HyperloopTT." HyperloopTT, www.hyperlooptt.com.

128. Angie Schmitt (2018). "Elon Musk's Tunnel Project in Los Angeles is
Bad Joke." StreetBlog USA, https://usa.streetsblog.org/2018/12/19/elon
-musks-tunnel-project-in-los-angeles-is-bad-joke/.

129. TBC (2020). "Projects." The Boring Company, www.boringcompany.com
/projects.

130. HyperloopTT (2020). "Projects." HyperloopTT, www.hyperlooptt.com
/projects.

131. Catherine L. Taylor, David J. Hyde, and Lawrence C. Barr (2016). *Hyperloop
Commercial Feasibility Analysis: High Level Overview.* National Aeronautics
and Space Administration, https://rosap.ntl.bts.gov/view/dot/12308.

132. PPIAF (2016). *Understanding Traffic Risk and Traffic Forecasting.* World
Bank Group, https://ppiaf.org/documents/4358/download.

133. Kent Hymel (2019). "If You Build It, They Will Drive: Measuring Induced
Demand for Vehicle Travel in Urban Areas." *Transport Policy, 76*, pp. 57–66,
https://doi.org/10.1016/j.tranpol.2018.12.006.

134. Taylor, Hyde, and Barr (2016), *Hyperloop Commercial Feasibility Analysis.*

135. Meredith Rutland Bauer (2019). "What Will Hyperloop Mean for Climate,
Ecosystems and Resources?" GreenBiz, www.greenbiz.com/article/what
-will-hyperloop-mean-climate-ecosystems-and-resources.

136. NASA (2020). "Advanced Air Mobility." National Aeronautics and Space
Administration, www.nasa.gov/aam.

137. Frederic Lardinois (2019). "A First Look at Amazon's New Delivery Drone."
Tech Crunch, https://tcrn.ch/2BpczSc.

138. Linda Lacina (2020). "The Next Big Disruption Is Coming. How Cities
Can Prepare For 'Flying Cars.'" World Economic Forum, www.weforum.org
/agenda/2020/09/flying-cars-are-the-next-big-disruption-how-cities-can
-prepare/.

139. Lee Williams (2020). "Future Transport: In the Skies and on the Ground."
Engineering and Technology https://eandt.theiet.org/content/articles/2020
/07/future-transport-in-the-skies-and-on-the-ground.

140. CRS (2018). *Supersonic Passenger Flights.* Congressional Research Service
https://fas.org/sgp/crs/misc/R45404.pdf; Paul Sillers (2020). "How Soon
Will Supersonic Jets Return to Our Skies?" CNN, https://cnn.it/2RJecib.

141. Kate Kelland (2019). "Drones to Deliver Vaccines, Blood and Drugs across
Ghana." Reuters https://reut.rs/32CBxHk.

142. Amazon (2016). "First Prime Air Delivery." Amazon Prime Air, https:
//amzn.to/31CojLk.

143. Nick Zazulia (2019). "The Air Taxi Challenges Uber Isn't Considering."
Aviation Today, www.aviationtoday.com/2019/04/23/the-challenges-uber
-isnt-thinking-about/.

144. Howard Slutsken (2019). "What It Was Really Like to Fly on Concorde." CNN, https://cnn.it/30eCcid.

145. Ryan Browne (2019). "Flying Taxis Could Lift Off in Six Years—Here's How Much It'll Cost to Ride One." CNBC https://cnb.cx/3kSXYAA.

146. Kevin DeGood (2020). *Flying Cars Will Undermine Democracy and the Environment.* Center for American Progress, https://ampr.gs/3h3f0cU.

147. Robert van der Linden (2004). "My Ride on the Concorde." *Air & Space Magazine,* www.airspacemag.com/flight-today/my-ride-on-the-concorde -6783087/.

148. Lambert (2020). "Uber and Hyundai Unveil New Electric Air Taxi." Electrek, https://electrek.co/2020/01/07/uber-hyundai-electric-air-taxi-evtol/.

149. EC (2019). *Implementing Regulation 2019/947 on the Rules and Procedures for the Operation of Unmanned Aircraft.* OJ L 152, European Commission, pp. 45–71, https://eur-lex.europa.eu/legal-content/EN/TXT/PDF/?uri =OJ:L:2019:152:FULL&from=EN.

150. Thomas Kirschstein (2020). "Comparison of Energy Demands of Drone-Based and Ground-Based Parcel Delivery Services." *Transportation Research Part D, 78,* https://doi.org/10.1016/j.trd.2019.102209.

151. Dan Rutherford, Brandon Graver, and Chen Chen (2019). *Noise and Climate Impacts of an Unconstrained Commercial Supersonic Network.* International Council on Clean Transportation, https://theicct.org/publications/noise -climate-impacts-unconstrained-supersonics.

152. Aaron Cheng, Min-seok Pang, and Paul A. Pavlou (2020). "Mitigating Traffic Congestion: The Role of Intelligent Transportation Systems." *Information Systems Research,* https://doi.org/10.1287/isre.2019.0894.

153. FHWA (2018). "Value Pricing Program." Federal Highway Administration, https://ops.fhwa.dot.gov/congestionpricing/value_pricing/.

154. Linda Poon (2018). "The App That Pays You to Find a Smarter Commute." *Bloomberg CityLab,* https://bloom.bg/31oL04A.

155. FHWA (2006). "What Is Congestion Pricing?" Federal Highway Administration, https://ops.fhwa.dot.gov/publications/congestionpricing/sec 2.htm.

156. TRB (2020). *Emerging Challenges to Priced Managed Lanes.* NCHRP Synthesis 559, Transportation Research Board, www.nap.edu/download /25924.

157. Dirk Van Amelsfort and Viktoria Swedish (2015). *Introduction to Congestion Charging: A Guide for Practitioners in Developing Cities.* Asian Development Bank, https://openaccess.adb.org/handle/11540/4318.

158. Hannah Frishberg and Amy Plitt (2019). "Congestion Pricing in NYC, Explained." NY Curbed, https://ny.curbed.com/2018/3/14/17117204/new -york-congestion-pricing-cuomo-subway-uber.

159. Washington State Commute Trip Reduction Program, https://wsdot.wa .gov/transit/ctr/home.

160. Brianne Eby, Martha Roskowski, and Robert Puentes (2020). *Congestion Pricing in the United States: Principles for Developing a Viable Program to Advance Sustainability and Equity Goals.* Eno Center for Transportation, www.enotrans.org/eno-resources/enocongestionpricing.

161. CARB (2014). *Research on Effects of Transportation and Land Use-Related Policies.* California Air Resources Board, https://arb.ca.gov/cc/sb375/policies/policies.htm.

162. Eby, Roskowski, and Puentes (2020). *Congestion Pricing in the United States.*

163. CIVITAS (2019). "Policy Brief: Urban Freight Logistics." CIVITAS, https://civitas.eu/document/civitas-policy-brief-urban-freight-logistics-2019.

164. Jose Holguín-Veras et al. (2015). *Improving Freight System Performance in Metropolitan Areas: A Planning Guide.* National Cooperative Freight Research Program Report 33, Transportation Research Board, www.trb.org/Publications/Blurbs/172487.aspx.

165. Jean-Paul Rodrigue and Laetitia Dablanc (2020). "Freight Distribution Strategies for City Logistics." City Logistics: Concepts, Policy and Practice, https://globalcitylogistics.org/?page_id=113.

166. C. Kim and N. Bhatt (2019). *Modernizing Urban Freight Deliveries with Microhubs.* Pembina Institute, www.pembina.org/reports/microhubs-fact sheet-v4-online.pdf.

167. Sebastian Merkle (2020). *APCOA PARKING Aims to Use Car Parks Throughout Europe as Logistics Hubs.* Parking Network, www.parking-net.com/parking-news/apcoa/use-car-parks-as-logistics-hubs.

168. CIVITAS (2015). *Making Urban Freight Logistics More Sustainable.* CIVITAS, www.eltis.org/sites/default/files/trainingmaterials/civ_pol-an5_urban_web-1.pdf.

169. DHL (2020). "DHL and REEF Technology Launch Pilot to Use Ecofriendly Cargo Bikes for Deliveries in Downtown Miami." PR Newswire, https://prn.to/3gGlQ73.

170. Nina Nesterova et al. (2017). *Sustainability Analysis of CITYLAB Solutions.* CITYLAB Consortium, European Commission, www.citylab-project.eu/deliverables/D5_4.pdf.

Chapter 6

1. CARB (2010–2014). *Impacts of Transportation and Land Use-Related Policies.* California Air Resources Board, http://arb.ca.gov/cc/sb375/policies/policies.htm.

2. Brianne Eby, Martha Roskowski, and Robert Puentes (2020). *Congestion Pricing in the United States: Principles for Developing a Viable Program to Advance Sustainability and Equity Goals.* Eno Center for Transportation, www.enotrans.org/eno-resources/enocongestionpricing.

3. Thorsten Koska and Frederic Rudolph (2016). *The Role of Walking and Cycling in Reducing Congestion: A Portfolio of Measures*. FLOW Project, http://h2020-flow.eu/uploads/tx_news/FLOW_REPORT_-_Portfolio_of_Measures_v_06_web.pdf.

4. Todd Litman (2019). *Evaluating Public Transit Benefits and Costs*. Victoria Transport Policy Institute, www.vtpi.org/tranben.pdf.

5. Karel Martens (2016). *Transport Justice: Designing Fair Transportation Systems*. New York: Routledge.

6. Todd Litman (2018). *Evaluating Transportation Equity*. Victoria Transport Policy Institute, www.vtpi.org/equity.pdf.

7. NACTO (2020). *Designing Streets for Kids*. Global Designing Cities Initiative, National Association of City Transportation Officials, https://global designingcities.org/publication/designing-streets-for-kids/.

8. FIA (2017). "Building Sustainable Mobility for Women." FIA Foundation, www.fiafoundation.org/blog/2017/november/building-sustainable-mobility-for-women.

9. Yingling Fan et al. (2019). *Advancing Transportation Equity: Research and Practice*. Center for Transportation Studies, University of Minnesota, www.dot.state.mn.us/planning/program/advancing-transportation-equity/pdf/CTS%2019-08.pdf.

10. Jeffrey Brinkman and Jeffrey Lin (2019). *Freeway Revolts!* Working Paper 19-29, Federal Reserve Bank of Philadelphia, https://doi.org/10.21799/frbp.wp.2019.29.

11. Sagar Shah and Brittany Wong (2020). *Toolkit to Integrate Health and Equity Into Comprehensive Plans Using the Sustaining Places–Best Practices for Comprehensive Plans Framework*. American Planning Association, www.planning.org/publications/document/9201866.

12. Reid Ewing et al. (2014). "Relationship Between Urban Sprawl and Physical Activity, Obesity, and Morbidity—Update and Refinement." *Health & Place*, 26, pp. 118–26, https://doi.org/10.1016/j.healthplace.2013.12.008.

13. ITE (2020). "COVID-19 Resources." Institute of Transportation Engineers, www.ite.org/about-ite/covid-19-resources/?_zs=MHVdl&_zl=qbii1.

14. NACTO (2020). *Streets for Response; Streets for Recovery*. National Association of City Transportation Officials, https://nacto.org/publication/streets-for-pandemic-response-recovery.

15. Salim Furth (2020). "Automobiles Seeded the Massive Coronavirus Epidemic in New York City." Market Urbanism, https://marketurbanism.com/2020/04/19/automobiles-seeded-the-massive-coronavirus-epidemic-in-new-york-city.

16. UITP (2020). *Management of COVID-19 Guidelines for Public Transport Operators*. Union Internationale des Transports Publics (International Association of Public Transport) www.uitp.org/publications/management-of-covid-19-guidelines-for-public-transport-operators.

17. ITF (2020). *Good to Go? Assessing the Environmental Performance of New Mobility.* International Transport Forum, www.itf-oecd.org/sites/default/files /docs/environmental-performance-new-mobility.pdf.

18. Florian Knobloch et al. (2020). "Net Emission Reductions from Electric Cars and Heat Pumps in 59 World Regions Over Time." *Nature Sustainability,* Vol. 3, pp. 437–47, https://doi.org/10.1038/s41893-020-0488-7.

Chapter 7

1. SmartETFs (2019). *The Smart Transportation Revolution.* SmartETFs, www.smartetfs.com/wp-content/uploads/2019/11/SmartETFs-Smart -Transportation-Revolution-FINAL.pdf.

2. Kelly Fleming (2019). "Uber and Lyft Induced Congestion Give a Preview of Driverless Car Hell." Earther, https://earther.gizmodo.com/uber-and-lyft -induced-congestion-give-a-preview-of-driv-1838489742.

3. Marc Schlossberg and Heather Brinton (2020). *Matching the Speed of Technology with the Speed of Local Government: Developing Codes and Policies Related to the Possible Impacts of New Mobility on Cities.* National Institute for Transportation and Communities, https://doi.org/ 10.15760/trec.251.

4. Bruce Schaller (2018). *The New Automobility: Lyft, Uber and the Future of American Cities.* Schaller Consulting, www.schallerconsult.com/rideservices /automobility.pdf.

5. NACTO (2016). *Guidelines for Regulating Shared Micromobility.* National Association of City Transportation Officials, https://nacto.org/wp-content /uploads/2019/09/NACTO_Shared_Micromobility_Guidelines_Web.pdf.

6. Daniel Sperling (2018). *Three Revolutions: Steering Automated, Shared, and Electric Vehicles to a Better Future.* Washington, DC: Island Press.

7. NACTO (2020). *Blueprint for Autonomous Urbanism.* National Association of City Transportation Officials, https://nacto.org/publication/bau2.

8. Hana Creger, Joel Espino, and Alvaro S. Sanchez (2019). *Autonomous Vehicle Heaven or Hell? Creating a Transportation Revolution that Benefits All.* Greenline Institute, http://greenlining.org/wp-content/uploads/2019/01 /R4_AutonomousVehiclesReportSingle_2019_2.pdf.

9. Tom Cohen and Clémence Cavoli (2019). "Automated Vehicles: Exploring Possible Consequences of Government (non)intervention for Congestion and Accessibility." *Transport Reviews, 39*(1), pp. 129–51, https://doi.org/10 .1080/01441647.2018.1524401.

10. Stephen Goldsmith (2020). "An Impact Framework for the New Mobility." *Governing.* www.governing.com/community/An-Impact-Framework-for-the -New-Mobility.html.

11. TRB (2018). *Guide to Creating and Sustaining a Culture of Innovation for Departments of Transportation.* Transportation Research Board, https://doi .org/10.17226/25307.

12. Becky Steckler (2019). "Navigating New Mobility: Policy Approaches for Cities." Urbanism Next, www.urbanismnext.org/resources/navigating-new -mobility-policy-approaches-for-cities.

13. Seattle (2017). *New Mobility Playbook*. Seattle Department of Transportation, www.seattle.gov/Documents/Departments/SDOT/NewMobilityPro gram/NewMobility_Playbook_9.2017.pdf.

14. LADOT (2020). "Transportation Technology Action Plan." Los Angeles Department of Transportation, https://ladot.lacity.org/projects/transportation -technology.

15. Denver (2019). *2030 Mobility Choice Blueprint*. Denver Regional Council of Governments, www.mobilitychoiceblueprintstudy.com.

16. Schlossberg and Brinton (2020). *Matching the Speed of Technology with the Speed of Local Government*.

17. NACTO (2018). *Guidelines for the Regulation and Management of Shared Active Transportation*. National Association of City Transportation Official, https://nacto.org/wp-content/uploads/2018/07/NACTO-Shared-Active -Transportation-Guidelines.pdf.

18. VTPI (2020). "Online TDM Encyclopedia." Victoria Transport Policy Institute, www.vtpi.org/tdm.

19. SSTI (2018). *Modernizing Mitigation: A Demand-Centered Approach*. State Smart Transportation Initiative and the Mayors Innovation Project, https: //ssti.us/2018/09/24/modern-mitigation-a-demand-centered-approach -ssti-september-2018.

20. TUMI. "TUMI's Global Urban Mobility Challenge." Transformative Urban Mobility Initiative, www.transformative-mobility.org/campaigns/2nd-global -urban-mobility-challenge.

21. Texas A&M (2018). "How To Fix Congestion." Texas A&M Transportation Institute, https://policy.tti.tamu.edu/congestion/how-to-fix-congestion.

22. SF Planning (2018). "TDM Tool." San Francisco Planning GIS, https: //sfplanninggis.org/tdm/.

23. Mike Spack and Jonah Finkelstein (2014). *Travel Demand Management: An Analysis of the Effectiveness of TDM Plans*. Spack Consulting, www.mikeontraffic .com/wp-content/uploads/2014/01/TDM-Plan-Effectiveness-Study.pdf.

24. WSDOT. "Commute Trip Reduction Program." Washington State Department of Transportation, https://wsdot.wa.gov/transit/ctr/home.

25. Steven Spears, Marlon G. Boarnet, and Susan Handy (2013). *Policy Brief on the Impacts of Voluntary Travel Behavior Change Programs Based on a Review of the Empirical Literature*. For Research on Impacts of Transportation and Land Use–Related Policies, California Air Resources Board, http://arb.ca .gov/cc/sb375/policies/policies.htm.

26. Jennifer Dill and Cynthia Mohr (2010). *Long-Term Evaluation of Individualized Marketing Programs for Travel Demand Management*. Portland State University, https://nitc.trec.pdx.edu/research/project/160.

27. NACTO (2020). *Blueprint for Autonomous Urbanism*.

28. Gregory H. Shill (2020). "Should Law Subsidize Driving?" *New York University Law Review 498*. University of Iowa Legal Studies Research Paper No. 2019-03, https://ssrn.com/abstract=3345366.

29. Marlon G. Boarnet (2013). "The Declining Role of the Automobile and the Re-Emergence of Place in Urban Transportation: The Past Will Be Prologue." *Regional Science Policy and Practice, 5*, pp. 237–53, https://doi.org/10.1111/rsp3.12007.

30. GOPR (2018). *On Evaluating Transportation Impacts in CEQA*. Governor's Office of Planning and Research, http://opr.ca.gov/ceqa/updates/sb-743.

31. WSL (2008). *Adoption of Statewide Goals to Reduce Annual Per Capita Vehicle Miles Traveled by 2050.* Washington State Legislature, https://apps.leg.wa.gov/RCW/default.aspx?cite=47.01.440.

32. ACEEE (2019). "Sustainable Transportation Planning." American Council for an Energy Efficient Economy, https://database.aceee.org/city/sustainable-transportation-planning.

33. GOPR (2018). *On Evaluating Transportation Impacts in CEQA*. Governor's Office of Planning and Research, http://opr.ca.gov/ceqa/updates/sb-743.

34. OECD (2018). *Effective Carbon Rates 2018*. Organization for Economic Development and Cooperation, www.oecd.org/tax/tax-policy/effective-carbon-rates-2018-brochure.pdf.

35. FHWA (2009). *Economics: Pricing, Demand, and Economic Efficiency: A Primer*. Office of Transportation Management, Federal Highway Administration, https://ops.fhwa.dot.gov/publications/fhwahop08041/fhwahop08041.pdf.

36. Gregory Pierce and Donald Shoup (2013). "Getting the Prices Right: An Evaluation of Pricing Parking by Demand in San Francisco." *Journal of the American Planning Association, 79*(1), http://shoup.bol.ucla.edu/PricingParkingByDemand.pdf.

37. Allen Greenberg and Jay Evans (2017). *Comparing Greenhouse Gas Reductions and Legal Implementation Possibilities for Pay-to-Save Transportation Price-shifting Strategies and EPA's Clean Power Plan*. Presented to the Union of Concerned Scientists, www.vtpi.org/G&E_GHG.pdf.

38. Kathy Lindquist and Michel Wendt (2012). *Least Cost Planning in Transportation: Synthesis*. Strategic Planning Division, Washington State Department of Transportation, http://www.wsdot.wa.gov/NR/rdonlyres/9435282F-8135-4E70-B4FE-0459E573ACF0/0/SynthesisLeastCostPlanningFINAL41212.pdf.

39. Ryerson CBI (2019). "Better Transit Through On-Demand Tech?" Ryerson City Building Institute, https://archive.citybuildinginstitute.ca/2019/11/20/better-transit-through-on-demand-tech/.

40. Will Macht (2019). "Developers Reduce Parking via Car Sharing." *Urban Land*, https://urbanland.uli.org/development-business/developers-reduce-parking-via-car-sharing/.

41. FHWA (2014). *Nonmotorized Transportation Pilot Program: Continued Progress in Developing Walking and Bicycling Networks—May 2014 Report.* John A Volpe National Transportation Systems Center, USDOT, www.fhwa.dot.gov/environment/bicycle_pedestrian/ntpp/2014_report/hep14035.pdf.

42. Todd Litman (2019). *Transportation Cost and Benefit Analysis.* Victoria Transport Policy Institute, www.vtpi.org.

43. Maggie L. Grabow et al. (2011). "Air Quality and Exercise-Related Health Benefits from Reduced Car Travel in the Midwestern United States." *Environmental Health Perspectives,* http://dx.doi.org/10.1289/ehp.1103440.

44. Christopher E. Ferrell (2015). *The Benefits of Transit in the United States: A Review and Analysis of Benefit-Cost Studies.* Mineta Transportation, http://transweb.sjsu.edu/PDFs/research/1425-US-transit-benefit-cost-analysis-study.pdf.

45. Todd Litman (2020). *Evaluating Public Transit Benefits and Costs.* Victoria Transport Policy Institute, www.vtpi.org/tranben.pdf.

46. Matthew Roe and Craig Toocheck (2017). *Curb Appeal: Curbside Management Strategies for Improving Transit Reliability.* National Association of City Transportation Officials, https://nacto.org/tsdg/curb-appeal-whitepaper.

47. Barbara McCann (2013). *Completing Our Streets: The Transition to Safe and Inclusive Transportation Networks.* Washington, DC: Island Press.

48. NACTO (2016). *Global Street Design Guide.* National Association of City Transportation Officials, https://globaldesigningcities.org/publication/global-street-design-guide/.

49. ITE (2019). *Curbside Management Practitioners Guide.* Institute of Transportation Engineers, www.ite.org/technical-resources/topics/complete-streets/curbside-management-resources/.

50. Seattle DOT (2016). *Seattle 2035, Transportation Element.* City of Seattle, www.seattle.gov/Documents/Departments/OPCD/OngoingInitiatives/SeattlesComprehensivePlan/Seattle2035_Transportation.pdf.

51. Haneen Khreis, Mark Nieuwenhuijsen, and Jeroen Bastiaanssen (2017). "Creating Car Free Cities: Rational, Requirements, Facilitators and Barriers." *Journal of Transport & Health,* pp. S65–S66, https://doi.org/10.1016/j.jth.2017.05.210.

52. Marc Schlossberg et al. (2018). *Rethinking the Street in an Era of Driverless Cars.* Urbanisim Next, https://urbanismnext.uoregon.edu/2018/01/25/new-report-rethinking-the-street-in-an-era-of-driverless-cars/.

53. Jeffrey Rosenblum, Anne W. Hudson, and Eran Ben-Joseph (2020). "Parking Futures: An International Review of Trends and Speculation." *Land Use Policy, 91,* https://doi.org/10.1016/j.landusepol.2019.104054.

54. Strong Towns (2020). "End Parking Minimums," www.strongtowns.org/parking.

55. Todd Litman (2016). *Parking Management: Strategies, Evaluation and Planning.* Victoria Transport Policy Institute, www.vtpi.org/park_man.pdf.

56. David Baker and Brad Leibin (2018). "Toward Zero Parking: Challenging Conventional Wisdom for Multifamily." *Urban Land*, https://urbanland.uli .org/economy-markets-trends/toward-zero-parking-challenging-conven tional-wisdom-multifamily-developments/.

57. Daniel Rowe et al. (2013). "Do Land Use, Transit and Walk Access Affect Residential Parking Demand?" *ITE Journal, 83*(2), pp. 24–28, http://metro .kingcounty.gov/up/projects/right-size-parking/pdf/ite-journal-feb-2013 -drowe.pdf.

58. NACTO (2020). *Blueprint for Autonomous Urbanism.*

59. John R. Quain (2019). "Eyes on the Road! (Your Car Is Watching)." *New York Times,* https://nyti.ms/2YfVCBR.

60. LADOT (2020). "Transportation Technology Action Plan."

61. ITF (2020). *Safe Micromobility.* International Transport Forum, www.itf -oecd.org/sites/default/files/docs/safe-micromobility_1.pdf.

62. Polis (2019). *Macro Managing Micro Mobility: Taking the Long View on Short Trips.* POLIS, www.eltis.org/in-brief/news/polis-releases-discussion-paper -shared-micromobility.

63. Collin Roughton et al. (2012). *Creating Walkable and Bikeable Communities: A User Guide to Developing Pedestrian and Bicycle Master Plans.* Center for Transportation Studies at Portland State University, https://ppms.trec.pdx .edu/media/project_files/IBPI%20Master%20Plan%20Handbook%20 FINAL.pdf.

64. METRO (2015). *Climate Smart Strategy for the Portland Metropolitan Region.* Portland Metro, www.oregonmetro.gov/climate-smart-strategy.

65. Sam Schwartz (2012). *Steps to a Walkable Community: A Guide for Citizens, Planners, and Engineers.* America Walks, www.americawalks.org/walksteps.

66. NACTO (2016). *Guidelines for Regulating Shared Micromobility.* National Association of City Transportation Officials, https://nacto.org/wp-content /uploads/2019/09/NACTO_Shared_Micromobility_Guidelines_Web.pdf.

67. Carlton Reid (2020). "Paris to Create 650 Kilometers of Post-Lockdown Cycleways." *Forbes,* www.forbes.com/sites/carltonreid/2020/04/22/paris -to-create-650-kilometers-of-pop-up-corona-cycleways-for-post-lockdown -travel/?sh=6f4ac14754d4.

68. Torsha Bhattacharya, Kevin Mills, and Tiffany Mulally (2019). *Active Transportation Transforms America: The Case for Increased Public Investment in Walking and Biking Connectivity.* Rails-to-Trails Conservancy, www.rails totrails.org/media/847675/activetransport_2019-report_finalreduced.pdf.

69. GHSA (2020). *Understanding and Tackling Micromobility: Transportation's New Disruptor.* Governor's Highway Safety Association, www.ghsa.org/sites /default/files/2020-08/GHSA_MicromobilityReport_Final_1.pdf.

70. Susan Shaheen and Adam Cohen (2019). *Shared Micromoblity Policy Toolkit: Docked and Dockless Bike and Scooter Sharing.* UC Berkeley, https://e scholarship.org/uc/item/00k897b5.

71. NACTO (2020). *Streets for Pandemic Response and Recovery.* National Association of City Transportation Officials, https://nacto.org/publication /streets-for-pandemic-response-recovery/.

72. C40 (2020). "Prioritising Cyclists and Pedestrians for a Safer, Stronger Recovery." C40 Knowledge Hub, www.c40knowledgehub.org/s/article /Prioritising-cyclists-and-pedestrians-for-a-safer-stronger-recovery?language =en_US.

73. NACTO (2018). *Bike Share and Shared Micromobility Initiative.* National Association of City Transportation Officials, https://nacto.org/program /bike-share-initiative.

74. Will Macht (2019). "Developers Reduce Parking via Car Sharing." *Urban Land,* https://urbanland.uli.org/development-business/developers-reduce -parking-via-car-sharing/?submitted=true.

75. Christopher Moon-Miklaucic et al. (2019). *The Evolution of Bike Sharing: 10 Questions on the Emergence of New Technologies, Opportunities, and Risks.* World Resources Institute, www.wri.org/publication/evolution-bike-sharing.

76. Sharon Feigon and Colin Murphy (2016). *Shared Mobility and the Transformation of Public Transit.* TCRP 188, Transit Cooperative Research Program, National Academies Press, https://doi.org/10.17226/23578.

77. SUMC (2019). *Equity and Shared Mobility Services. Working with the Private Sector to Meet Equity Objectives,* Shared-Use Mobility Center, https://se cureservercdn.net/45.40.148.147/6c6.77f.myftpupload.com/wp-content /uploads/2019/12/EquitySharedMobilityServices-FINAL.pdf.

78. NUMO (2020). *New Mobility Atlas.* New Urban Mobility Alliance, www .numo.global/spotlight-on/micromobility/numo-new-mobility-atlas.

79. NACTO (2019). *Shared Micromobility in the U.S.: 2018.* National Association of City Transportation Officials, https://nacto.org/shared-micromo bility-2018/National.

80. NACTO (2020). *Bike Share in the U.S.: 2010–2016.* National Association of City Transportation Officials, https://nacto.org/bike-share-statistics-2016.

81. Susan Shaheen and Adam Cohen (2019). *Shared Micromoblity Policy Toolkit: Docked and Dockless Bike and Scooter Sharing.* Transportation Sustainability Research Center, https://doi.org/10.7922/G2TH8JW7.

82. Dean Yobbi (2020). "Pandemic Boosts Share-Bike and Scooter Business." *Bicycle Retailer,* www.bicycleretailer.com/industry-news/2020/08/10/pan demic-boosts-share-bike-and-scooter-business#.X62AulNKg1J.

83. NACTO (2020). *Shared Micromobility in the U.S.* National Association of City Transportation Officials, https://nacto.org/shared-micromobility-2019.

84. PBT (2019). *2018 E-Scooter Findings Report.* Portland Bureau of Transportation, www.portlandoregon.gov/transportation/article/709719.

85. Matt Daus (2018). "A World Tour of For-Hire and TNC Regulation." Chauffeur Driven, www.chauffeurdriven.com/news-features/in-this-issue/1897-a -world-tour-of-for-hire-and-tnc-regulation.html.

86. Schlossberg and Brinton (2020). *Matching the Speed of Technology with the Speed of Local Government.*

87. UCS (2020). *Ride-Hailing's Climate Risks: Steering a Growing Industry Toward a Clean Transportation Future.* Union of Concerned Scientists, www .ucsusa.org/resources/ride-hailing-climate-risks.

88. ITF (2016). *The Shared-Use City: Managing the Curb.* International Transport Forum, www.itf-oecd.org/sites/default/files/docs/shared-use-city-man aging-curb.pdf.

89. Rex Deighton-Smith (2018). *The Economics of Regulating Ride-Hailing and Dockless Bike Share.* International Transport Forum, www.itf-oecd.org/sites /default/files/docs/economics-regulating-ride-hailing-dockeless-bike-share .pdf.

90. Schaller (2018). *New Automobility.*

91. Becky Steckler (2019). "Navigating New Mobility."

92. Eric Zimmer (2019). "City Council Gives Green Light for Ride-hailing Companies to Operate in Vancouver." *Daily Hive,* https://dailyhive.com/van couver/vancouver-ride-hailing-operation.

93. Ricardo (2020). *Determining the Environmental Impacts of Conventional and Alternatively Fuelled Vehicles Through LCA.* European Commission, https: //ec.europa.eu/clima/sites/clima/files/transport/vehicles/docs/2020 _study_main_report_en.pdf.

94. Shihping Kevin Huang, Lopin Kuo, and Kuei-lan Chou (2018). "The Impacts of Government Policies on Green Utilization Diffusion and Social Benefits—A Case Study of Electric Motorcycles in Taiwan." *Energy Policy, 119,* pp. 473–86.

95. Ryan C. Bosworth, Grant Patty, and Matthew Crabtree (2017). *The Current State of Electric Vehicle Subsidies: Economic, Environmental, and Distributional Impacts.* Strata, https://strata.org/pdf/2017/ev-full.pdf.

96. David A. Hensher (2020). "Electric Cars—They May in Time Increase Car Use Without Effective Road Pricing Reform and Risk Lifecycle Carbon Emission Increases." *Transport Reviews, 40*(3), 265–66, https://doi.org/10 .1080/01441647.2020.1709273.

97. Dunsky Energy Consulting (2020). *City of Toronto Electric Vehicle Strategy.* City of Toronto, www.toronto.ca/wp-content/uploads/2020/02/8c46 -City-of-Toronto-Electric-Vehicle-Strategy.pdf.

98. Carolyn Fortuna (2020). "Connecticut Targets Lower Income Buyers With New Clean Vehicle Subsidies." Clean Technica, https://cleantechnica.com /2020/09/13/connecticut-targets-lower-income-buyers-with-new-clean -vehicle-subsidies/.

99. PIBC (2017). *Automated and Connected Vehicles, Pedestrians, and Bicyclists.* Pedestrian and Bicycle Information Center, www.pedbikeinfo.org/cms/down loads/PBIC_AV_Discussion_Guide.pdf.

100. NACTO (2020). *Blueprint for Autonomous Urbanism.*

101. Steckler (2019). "Navigating New Mobility."

102. NACTO (2020). *Blueprint for Autonomous Urbanism.*
103. Schlossberg and Brinton (2020). *Matching the Speed of Technology with the Speed of Local Government.*
104. Mobility Lab (2019). *Market Research on Real Time Transit Information Needs and Users' Expectations.* Mobility Lab, https://mobilitylab.org/research-document/market-research-on-real-time-transit-information-needs-and-users-expectations/.
105. Roe and Toocheck (2017). *Curb Appeal.*
106. World Bank (2018). *TOD Implementation Resources and Tools.* Global Platform for Sustainable Cities; World Bank, http://hdl.handle.net/10986/31121.
107. ITF (2012). *Towards Seamless Public Transport.* International Transport Forum, www.internationaltransportforum.org/jtrc/PolicyBriefs/PDFs/2012-12-10.pdf.
108. Alice Grossman and Romic Aevaz (2020). *MOD Fare Integration for Transit.* Eno Foundation, www.enotrans.org/eno-resources/modfareintegration/.
109. Dario Hidalgo and Aileen Carrigan (2010). *Modernizing Public Transportation: Lessons Learned from Major Bus Improvements in Latin America and Asia.* EMBARQ, www.embarq.org/sites/default/files/EMB2010_BRT REPORT.pdf.
110. TC (2019). "There's a Reason Transit Ridership Is Rising in These 7 Cities." Transit Center, https://transitcenter.org/theres-a-reason-transit-ridership-is-rising-in-these-7-cities.
111. Hiroaki Suzuki, Robert Cervero, and Kanako Iuchi (2013). *Transforming Cities with Transit: Transport and Land Use Integration for Sustainable Urban Development.* Urban Development Series, World Bank, https://doi.org/10.1596/978-0-8213-9745-9.
112. ITDP (2012). "The Bus Rapid Transit Standard." Institute for Transportation and Development Policy, www.itdp.org/library/standards-and-guides/the-bus-rapid-transit-standard/.
113. G. B. Arrington et al. (2008). *Effects of TOD on Housing, Parking, and Travel.* Report 128, Transit Cooperative Research Program, www.trb.org/Publications/Blurbs/160307.aspx.
114. Transit Center (2020). "How Transit Agencies Are Responding to the COVID-19 Public Health Threat." https://transitcenter.org/how-transit-agencies-are-responding-to-the-covid-19-public-health-threat/.
115. Maxine Joselow (2020). "There Is Little Evidence That Mass Transit Poses a Risk of Coronavirus Outbreaks." *Scientific American*, www.scientificamerican.com/article/there-is-little-evidence-that-mass-transit-poses-a-risk-of-coronavirus-outbreaks/.
116. Yale Z. Wong, David A. Hensher, and Corinne Mulley (2020). "Mobility as a Service (MaaS): Charting a Future Context." *Transportation Research Part A: Policy and Practice, 131*, pp. 5–19, https://doi.org/10.1016/j.tra.2019.09.030.

117. UITP (2019). *Mobility as a Service Report*. International Association of Public Transport, www.uitp.org.

118. MA (2020). *MaaS Guide*. MaaS Alliance, https://maas.guide.

119. Deighton-Smith (2018). *Economics of Regulating Ride-Hailing and Dockless Bike Share*.

120. Tammy D. Allen, Timothy D. Golden, and Kristen Shockley (2016). "How Effective Is Telecommuting? Assessing the Status of Our Scientific Findings." *Psychological Science in the Public Interest, 16*(2), pp. 40–68, https://doi.org/10.1177/1529100615593273.

121. Kian Williams (2020). "COVID-19: Cities and Municipal Broadband." Econsult, https://econsultsolutions.com/covid-19-cities-municipal-broadband/.

122. Kevin DeGood (2020). "Flying Cars Will Undermine Democracy and the Environment." Center for American Progress, https://ampr.gs/3h3f0cU.

123. WEF (2020). "Principles of the Urban Sky." World Economic Forum, www.weforum.org/reports/principles-of-the-urban-sky.

124. Ken Dunlap and Paul Lewis (2020). *Bridging the Gap: Sustaining UAS Progress While Pursuing a Permanent Regulatory Framework*. Eno Center for Transportation, www.enotrans.org/wp-content/uploads/2020/08/Bridging-the-Gap-Sustaining-UAS-Progress-While-Pursuing-a-Regulatory-Framework.pdf.

125. Texas A&M (2018). "How to Fix Congestion."

126. TRB (2020). *Emerging Challenges to Priced Managed Lanes*. NCHRP Synthesis 559, Transportation Research Board, https://doi.org/10.17226/25924.

127. Dirk Van Amelsfort and Viktoria Swedish (2015). *Introduction to Congestion Charging: A Guide for Practitioners in Developing Cities*. Asian Development Bank and the Deutsche Gesellschaft für Internationale Zusammenarbeit, https://openaccess.adb.org/handle/11540/4318.

128. World Bank and IRU (2017). *Road Freight Transport Services Reform: Guiding Principles for Practitioners and Policy Makers*. World Bank and IRU, www.iru.org/sites/default/files/2017-01/iru-world-bank-road-freight-transport-services-reform-en.pdf.

129. Jose Holguín-Veras et al. (2015). *Improving Freight System Performance in Metropolitan Areas: A Planning Guide*. National Cooperative Freight Research Program Report 33, Transportation Research Board, www.trb.org/Publications/Blurbs/172487.aspx.

130. Christopher Lamm et al. (2017). *Guide for Integrating Goods and Services Movement by Commercial Vehicles in Smart Growth Environments*. National Cooperative Highway Research Program, Research Report 844, TRB, www.trb.org/Main/Blurbs/175482.aspx.

131. Oliver Lah (2016). "Sharing Opportunities for Low Carbon Urban Transportation." Wuppertal Institut, https://wupperinst.org/en/p/wi/p/s/pd/471.

132. CIVITAS (2015). *Making Urban Freight Logistics More Sustainable.* CIVITAS, www.eltis.org/sites/default/files/trainingmaterials/civ_pol-an5_urban _web-1.pdf.

Chapter 8

1. Affordability is defined as households spending less than 45 percent of their budget on housing and transportation combined (*Housing and Transportation Affordability Index*, https://htaindex.cnt.org). Since most households spend about 35 percent of their budget on housing, this leaves 10 percent for transportation.
2. SGA (2020). *What Are Complete Streets?* Smart Growth America, https: //smartgrowthamerica.org/category/complete-streets.
3. World Bank (2013). *Improving Accessibility to Transport for People with Limited Mobility: A Practical Guidance Note.* World Bank, http://documents 1.worldbank.org/curated/en/575221468278939280/pdf/Accessibility 0Report0Final.pdf.
4. WHO (2020). *Supporting Healthy Urban Transport and Mobility in the Context of COVID-19.* World Health Organization, https://apps.who.int/iris /handle/10665/336264.
5. NACTO (2020). *Rapid Response: Tools for Cities.* National Association of City Transportation Officials, https://nacto.org/covid19-rapid-response-tools -for-cities.
6. Salim Furth (2020). *Automobiles Seeded the Massive Coronavirus Epidemic in New York City.* Market Urbanism, https://marketurbanism.com /2020/04/19/automobiles-seeded-the-massive-coronavirus-epidemic-in -new-york-city.
7. Despacio and ITDP (2013). *Practical Guidebook: Parking and Travel Demand Management Policies in Latin America.* Despacio and Institute for Transportation and Development Policy for the InterAmerican Development Bank, https://itdpdotorg.wpengine.com/wp-content/uploads/2014 /07/Practical_Guidebook-_Parking_and_Travel_Demand_Management _Policies_in_Latin_America.pdf.

Page numbers in *italics* indicate photos and illustrations. Page numbers in **bold** indicate tables and charts.

TODD LITMAN

Todd Litman is founder and executive director of the Victoria Transport Policy Institute, an independent research organization dedicated to developing innovative solutions to transport problems. His work helps expand the range of impacts and options considered in transportation decision-making, improve evaluation methods, and make specialized technical concepts accessible to a larger audience. His research is used worldwide in transport planning and policy analysis. Mr. Litman has worked on numerous studies that evaluate transportation costs, benefits, and innovations. He has served as a consultant for a diverse range of clients, including government agencies, professional organizations, developers, and nongovernmental organizations. He has worked in more than two dozen countries, on every continent except Antarctica. He is active in several professional organizations, including the Institute of Transportation Engineers (ITE) and the Transportation Research Board.